I0448192

February 2013

SUB-SAHARAN AFRICA

Trends in U.S. and Chinese Economic Engagement

GAO
Accountability ★ Integrity ★ Reliability

GAO-13-199

GAO
Accountability * Integrity * Reliability
Highlights

Highlights of GAO-13-199, a report to congressional requesters

SUB-SAHARAN AFRICA

Trends in U.S. and Chinese Economic Engagement

Why GAO Did This Study

Since 2001, China has rapidly increased its economic engagement with sub-Saharan African countries. The United States has increased aid to sub-Saharan Africa and in 2010 provided more than a quarter of all U.S. international economic assistance to the region. According to some observers, China's foreign assistance and investments in Africa have been driven in part by the desire for natural resources and stronger diplomatic relations. Some U.S. officials and other stakeholders also have questioned whether China's activities affect U.S. interests in the region.

GAO was asked to review the nature of the United States' and China's engagement in sub-Saharan Africa. This report examines (1) goals and policies in sub-Saharan Africa; (2) trade, grants and loans, and investment activities in the region; and (3) engagement in three case-study countries—Angola, Ghana, and Kenya. GAO obtained information from, among others, 11 U.S. agencies, U.S. firms, and host-government officials. GAO was not able to meet with Chinese officials. GAO did not include U.S. and Chinese security engagement in the scope of this study.

View GAO-13-199. To view a supplemental report with more details on case-study countries see GAO-13-280SP. For more information, contact David Gootnick at (202) 512-3149 or gootnickd@gao.gov.

What GAO Found

The United States and China have emphasized different policies and approaches for their engagement with sub-Saharan Africa. U.S. goals have included strengthening democratic institutions, supporting human rights, using development assistance to improve health and education, and helping sub-Saharan African countries build global trade. The Chinese government, in contrast, has stated the goal of establishing closer ties with African countries by seeking mutual benefit for China and African nations and by following a policy of noninterference in countries' domestic affairs.

Both the United States and China have seen sharp growth in trade with sub-Saharan Africa over the past decade, with China's total trade in goods increasing faster and surpassing U.S. trade in 2009. Petroleum imports constitute the majority of U.S. and Chinese imports from sub-Saharan Africa, with China also importing a large amount of other natural resources. China's exports of goods to the region have grown and far exceed U.S. exports of goods. Information on other key aspects of China's engagement in sub-Saharan Africa is limited in some cases, since China does not publish comprehensive data on its foreign assistance or government-sponsored loans to the region. Data-collection efforts focused on specific countries, as GAO's case-study analysis shows, can provide further insights but do not fully eliminate these information gaps.

U.S. and Chinese Imports from, and Exports to, Sub-Saharan Africa, 2001 and 2011

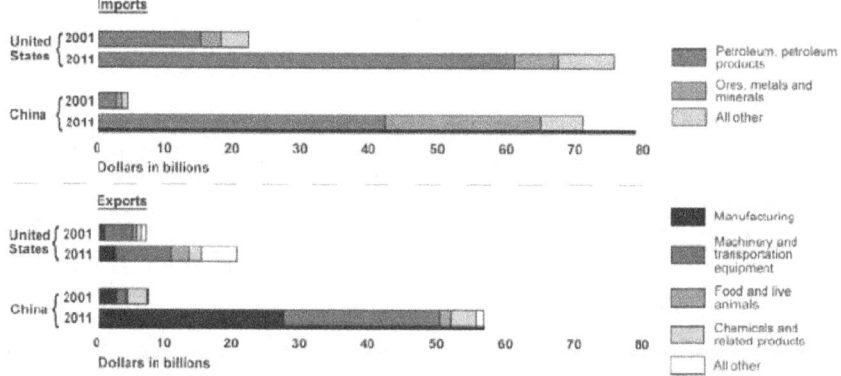

Source: GAO analysis of UN data.

Both the United States and China chiefly import natural resources from sub-Saharan Africa, but data from Angola, Ghana, and Kenya suggest that U.S. and Chinese patterns of engagement have differed in other respects. The United States has primarily provided grants to Kenya for health and humanitarian programs. Data from Ghana and Kenya suggest that China has provided much smaller amounts of grant assistance and pursued increasing engagement through loans for large-scale infrastructure projects. Information from Angola, Ghana, and Kenya indicates that direct competition between U.S. and Chinese firms is limited, with U.S. firms concentrated in higher-technology areas. Further, differences across the three countries suggest that host-government requirements, such as regulations on hiring local labor, influence Chinese and U.S. firms' engagement in each case-study country.

_____ **United States Government Accountability Office**

Contents

Abbreviations

AGOA	African Growth and Opportunity Act
BEA	Bureau of Economic Analysis
Commerce	Department of Commerce
China Ex-Im	Export-Import Bank of China
FOCAC	Forum on China-Africa Cooperation
GDP	gross domestic product
GSP	Generalized System of Preferences
IMF	International Monetary Fund
MCC	Millennium Challenge Corporation
NGO	nongovernmental organization
OECD	Organization for Economic Cooperation and Development
OPIC	Overseas Private Investment Corporation
State	Department of State
Treasury	Department of the Treasury
UN	United Nations
USAID	U.S. Agency for International Development
U.S. Ex-Im	Export-Import Bank of the United States
USTR	Office of the U.S. Trade Representative

United States Government Accountability Office
Washington, DC 20548

February 7, 2013

The Honorable James M. Inhofe
United States Senate

The Honorable Jack Kingston
House of Representatives

China's economic ties with sub-Saharan Africa, including its rapidly rising trade and investment in the region, have drawn global attention. While U.S. trade with the region has also increased, the United States has generally focused on providing development and humanitarian assistance to African countries, directing more than a quarter of its foreign economic assistance to the region in 2010. Since 2001, China has substantially increased its economic engagement with sub-Saharan African countries, with strong growth in both imports and exports. According to some observers, China's foreign assistance and investments throughout Africa since that time have been driven in part by the Chinese government's desire to obtain a share in Africa's natural resources as well as by its interest in establishing diplomatic relations with countries in the region. Various U.S. officials and members of the U.S. business community have questioned whether China's role in the region is affecting U.S. interests and opportunities for U.S. firms in sub-Saharan Africa.

You asked us to review the nature of the United States' and China's engagement in sub-Saharan Africa.[1] This report examines (1) U.S. and Chinese goals and policies for sub-Saharan Africa; (2) the United States' and China's trade, grants and loans, and investment activities in sub-Saharan Africa; and (3) aspects of the United States' and China's engagement in three sub-Saharan African countries—Angola, Ghana, and Kenya.

To review U.S. and Chinese goals and policies with respect to sub-Saharan Africa, we used U.S. government documents, publicly available Chinese government documents, and statements from U.S. government

---

[1]This review was conducted in response to a request from Representative Jack Kingston and Senator James Inhofe—then Ranking Member, Senate Foreign Relations Subcommittee on East Asian and Pacific Affairs—to review U.S. and Chinese engagement in sub-Saharan Africa.

officials. To examine the United States' and China's engagement through trade, grants and loans, and investment in sub-Saharan Africa, we analyzed available data for the United States and China from a variety of U.S., multilateral, and Chinese government sources,[2] generally for 2001 through 2010 or 2011.[3] We did not include security issues within the scope of this study. To identify the best available data, as well as data limitations, we interviewed U.S. government officials and experts in Washington, D.C. We also analyzed information on U.S. programs and funding from the U.S. Department of Commerce (Commerce), the Millennium Challenge Corporation (MCC), the Overseas Private Investment Corporation (OPIC), the Export-Import Bank of the United States (U.S. Ex-Im), and the U.S. Agency for International Development (USAID). In addition, we analyzed publicly available information from Chinese government entities, such as the Ministry of Commerce; the World Bank; the International Monetary Fund (IMF); and scholarly literature, among other sources, and we obtained some data from case-study country governments. To compare in depth the nature of the United States' and China's engagement in sub-Saharan Africa, we conducted case studies of Angola, Ghana, and Kenya. We selected these countries on the basis of our assessment of the levels, types, and intersection of the United States' and China's engagement in trade, grants and loans, and investment activity in each country; the three countries' geographic diversity; and input from U.S. government officials and experts on China's role in Africa. These case studies are meant to be illustrative and are not generalizable. We conducted work in Washington, D.C., and in Angola, Ghana, and Kenya, including meetings with officials from U.S. agencies, host-government ministries, U.S. businesses, other donors, and nongovernmental organizations (NGO). Despite our requests, we were unable to meet with Chinese government officials in Africa or in

---

[2]The data sources we identified include trade data from the United Nations (UN) Commodity Trade database, the U.S. Department of Commerce's (Commerce) Trade Policy Information System, and Commerce's Bureau of Economic Analysis (BEA); aid data from the U.S. Agency for International Development (USAID) and scholars; loan and other financing data from the Export-Import Bank of the United States (U.S. Ex-Im) and Overseas Private Investment Corporation (OPIC); and investment data from BEA and China's Ministry of Commerce.

[3]When data were unavailable for this period, we used data for shorter periods. For comparability, and given challenges in determining appropriate deflators for some data, we used nominal rather than inflation-adjusted values for data on trade, grants and loans, and investments. All information sources reported nominal data in U.S. dollars. All of the data we report are for calendar years, except where noted otherwise.

Washington, D.C. We have noted data limitations as appropriate, such as lack of available data on China's grants and loans to the region and likely underreporting of China's investment data. Overall, we determined the data presented in this study to be generally reliable for the purposes for which they are used. Appendix I provides a more detailed discussion of our objectives, scope, and methodology. Additional information on the United States' and China's trade, grants and loans, and investment activities in Angola, Ghana, and Kenya is presented in a separate supplemental report, GAO-13-280SP.

We conducted this performance audit from November 2011 to February 2013 in accordance with generally accepted government auditing standards. Those standards require that we plan and perform the audit to obtain sufficient, appropriate evidence to provide a reasonable basis for our findings and conclusions based on our audit objectives. We believe that the evidence obtained provides a reasonable basis for our findings and conclusions based on our audit objectives.

Background

Sub-Saharan Africa comprises 49 countries,[4] including 4 of the 10 economies worldwide that grew most rapidly from 2001 through 2011.[5] Since 1990, overall decreases in maternal and child mortality rates, as well as improvements in indicators measuring education and poverty rates, have shown that economic and social conditions are improving in the region. However, countries in sub-Saharan Africa, including our three case-study countries—Angola, Ghana, and Kenya—continue to face significant development challenges, such as those related to governance and government transparency, and overall low income levels.

Figure 1 shows the location and selected characteristics of the sub-Saharan Africa region and our case-study countries.

---

[4]Data in this report generally do not include South Sudan, which gained independence in July 2011.

[5]The four countries are Angola, Chad, Equatorial Guinea, and Sierra Leone. Analysis of economic growth was based on the World Bank's data on annual gross domestic product (GDP) growth from 2001 through 2011.

Figure 1: Selected Economic and Development Indicators for Sub-Saharan Africa Compared with Angola, Ghana, and Kenya

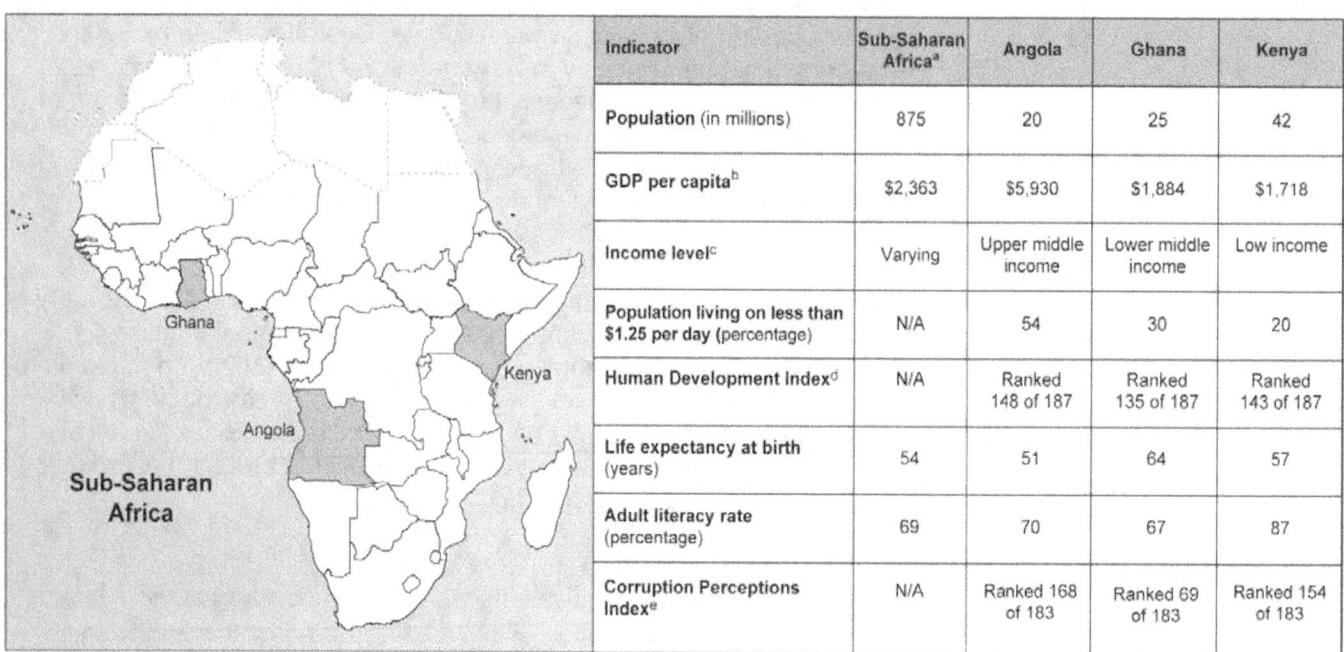

Indicator	Sub-Saharan Africa[a]	Angola	Ghana	Kenya
Population (in millions)	875	20	25	42
GDP per capita[b]	$2,363	$5,930	$1,884	$1,718
Income level[c]	Varying	Upper middle income	Lower middle income	Low income
Population living on less than $1.25 per day (percentage)	N/A	54	30	20
Human Development Index[d]	N/A	Ranked 148 of 187	Ranked 135 of 187	Ranked 143 of 187
Life expectancy at birth (years)	54	51	64	57
Adult literacy rate (percentage)	69	70	67	87
Corruption Perceptions Index[e]	N/A	Ranked 168 of 183	Ranked 69 of 183	Ranked 154 of 183

Source: GAO analysis of data from the World Bank, United Nations, and Transparency International.

Note: Data shown are the most recent available.

[a]Some data sources did not consistently classify countries in sub-Saharan Africa. For example, data for sub-Saharan Africa from the Human Development Index did not include Sudan. In addition, some data were not available for the sub-Saharan Africa region.

[b]Gross domestic product (GDP) per capita is based on purchasing power parity, which equalizes the purchasing power of different currencies in their home countries by taking into account the relative cost of living and the inflation rates of different countries, rather than by comparing the countries' nominal GDP data.

[c]The World Bank classified income level by gross national income per capita as follows: low income, $1,025 or less; lower-middle income, $1,026 to $4,035; upper-middle income, $4,036 to $12,475; and high income, $12,476 or more.

[d]The Human Development Index provides a composite measure of three basic dimensions of human development: health, education, and income, where a ranking of 1 indicates a country with high social and economic development.

[e]Based on the perceived level of corruption of a country's public sector, where a ranking of 1 indicates the lowest level of perceived corruption relative to other countries included in the index.

- *Angola.* In 2002, Angola officially ended a 27-year civil war that resulted in the deaths of up to 1.5 million people and destroyed the country's infrastructure. Since 2001, Angola has become one of the largest crude oil-producing countries in sub-Saharan Africa, and high international oil prices have driven the country's high growth rate in recent years. The country's efforts to rebuild following the war spurred a construction boom and—although the country imports half of its food—an increased focus on agriculture. Despite Angola's oil reserves and relatively high income level per capita, the UN classifies Angola as a least developed country, on the basis of its low ratings on human development indicators and the weakness of its economy. More than 54 percent of Angola's population—the highest percentage among our three case-study countries—lives on the equivalent of less than $1.25 per day. In 2011, Transparency International ranked Angola's public sector among the most corrupt in sub-Saharan Africa, and other sources have noted significant challenges including corruption and lack of transparency, particularly in the extractive industries.[6]

- *Ghana.* In 1957, Ghana became the first sub-Saharan country in colonial Africa to gain its independence. Ghana's economy has generally been strengthened by a quarter century of relatively sound management, a competitive business environment, and sustained reductions in poverty levels. The country is well endowed with natural resources, and oil production that began in 2010 is expected to boost Ghana's economic growth. Agriculture accounts for roughly one-quarter of Ghana's gross domestic product (GDP) and employs half of the workforce. In 2011, the year that Ghana began to export oil, the World Bank elevated Ghana to lower-middle-income status based on its per capita income.[7]

- *Kenya.* Kenya is considered a hub for trade and finance in the East Africa region of sub-Saharan Africa and is that region's largest economy. Kenya's economic growth has been affected by increasing inflation, high energy and food prices, and the 2011 drought in the Horn of Africa. In addition, contested national elections in 2008 and the resulting violence negatively affected the economy and foreign

---

[6]Transparency International, *Corruption Perceptions Index 2011* (Berlin, Germany: 2011), 4-5.

[7]According to a report by the Center for Global Development, Ghana was able to achieve this change in income status relatively quickly as a result of rebasing its GDP in 2009. The GDP rebasing—a statistical adjustment to correct for some underreporting in national accounts—put Ghana in a new income category. Although the World Bank calculates income status on the basis of gross national income, the Center for Global Development report states that gross national income and GDP amounts do not differ significantly. Todd Moss and Stephanie Majerowicz, *No Longer Poor: Ghana's New Income Status and Implications of Graduation from IDA* (Washington, D.C.: Center for Global Development, 2012).

investments in Kenya. Although economic recovery continues, the country faces challenges including a growing trade imbalance, corruption, and rural and urban poverty. Kenya also faces challenges in its manufacturing and drought-affected agricultural sectors, which affect the country's economic stability. The overall welfare of Kenyans has improved in the past decade, with a general decline in national poverty and rising primary education enrollment rates. However, because of Kenya's low per-capita income levels, the World Bank classifies it as a low-income country. The World Bank has noted that poverty and climate change issues remain among the country's top development challenges.

U.S. and Chinese Economies

The United States is the world's largest trader in goods—that is, total imports and exports—and its market-based economy is the world's largest economy, producing one-fifth of total global economic output.[8] In addition, the United States is the largest exporter of services, primarily education services; financial services; and business, professional, and technical services, among others. As a member of the Organization for Economic Cooperation and Development (OECD), the United States collaborates with other countries and helps set international standards on economic, social, and scientific issues, to help member and nonmember countries promote economic growth, free markets, and efficient use of resources.[9] The United States also coordinates its development assistance activities with other members of the OECD Development Assistance Committee, a forum of many of the largest funders of aid that has a mandate to promote development cooperation and other policies for sustainable development. In accordance with the 2005 Paris Declaration on Aid Effectiveness, the U.S. government generally does not condition its aid on, or "tie" it to, the recipient country's use of the aid to procure goods or services from the United States.

---

[8]In 2011, U.S. GDP, based on purchasing power parity, was $15 trillion and U.S. per-capita GDP was approximately $48,400.

[9]OECD is an organization of 34 industrialized countries, operating by consensus, that fosters dialogue among members to discuss, develop, and refine economic and social policies and provides an arena for establishing multilateral agreements.

China is the world's largest manufacturer and exporter of goods,[10] with overall economic output second only to the United States'.[11] In 2010, China was the fourth-highest-ranked global exporter of services, although it still imports more services than it exports. Unlike the United States, China is not a member of OECD. However, China's entry into the World Trade Organization in 2001 has helped the country expand its economic integration with the global economy, and such integration is expected to help China increase its efficiency, innovation, and global competitiveness.[12] Over the past 3 decades, China has been transitioning from a rural, agricultural society to an urban, industrial society and from a planned economy, where the government makes key decisions about goods and production, toward one that is, like the U.S. economy, more market based. During this transformation, China's growth has been driven by manufacturing, in part because of its relatively low labor costs. However, China's overall growth has imposed increased pressure on the availability of natural resources. Moreover, according to a joint study by the World Bank and the Chinese government, state-owned enterprises are not yet clearly distinguished from the private sector.[13] This study notes that, more than in other economies, China's state-owned enterprises and government are closely connected and generally are

---

[10]See World Bank and People's Republic of China Development Research Center of the State Council, *China 2030: Building a Modern, Harmonious, and Creative High-Income Society* (Washington, D.C.: 2012). China's State Council is the highest executive and administrative entity in the Chinese government and oversees all major central government ministries, commissions, and other key state entities.

[11]In 2011, China's GDP, based on purchasing power parity, was $11.4 trillion, or about three-quarters of U.S. GDP; China's per-capita GDP was approximately $8,500, or one-sixth of U.S. per-capita GDP.

[12]See World Bank and People's Republic of China Development Research Center of the State Council, *China 2030*. After 15 years of negotiations to join the World Trade Organization, on December 11, 2001, China bound itself to open and liberalize its economy and offer a more predictable environment for trade and foreign investment in accordance with the organization's rules.

[13]World Bank and People's Republic of China Development Research Center of the State Council, *China 2030*.

mutually supportive and that China's large private enterprises also benefit from government financing and commercial diplomacy.[14]

Anticorruption Laws for U.S. and Chinese Firms

U.S. companies are subject to various regulations with respect to commercial activities abroad, including the Foreign Corrupt Practices Act of 1977, which prohibits payments to foreign government officials to assist in obtaining or retaining business.[15] The Foreign Corrupt Practices Act applies to all U.S. persons, including corporations, as well as foreign firms that issue securities regulated pursuant to the Securities Exchange Act of 1934. The United States also adopted the OECD Anti-Bribery Convention in 1998.[16] In 2011, the Chinese government amended its anticorruption laws to outlaw bribery of foreign public officials by Chinese nationals, companies, and residents for commercial benefit. Both the United States and China signed the United Nations Convention against Corruption in 2003.[17] According to Transparency International, in 2011, firms from China were perceived as among the most likely to pay bribes abroad, ranked at 27 among firms from 28 countries; U.S. firms, ranked at 10, were perceived as less likely to pay bribes abroad.[18]

[14]For example, state-owned enterprises in China will accept informal guidance from government officials and, in return, are more likely to receive preferential access to bank finance, privileged access to business opportunities, and even protection against competition. However, the study notes that more than one in four state-owned enterprises in China incurs a loss, and state-owned enterprises have exhibited lower growth in productivity than have private enterprises.

[15]Pub. L. No. 95-213, as amended (codified at 15 U.S.C. §§78dd-1 et seq).

[16]The OECD Anti-Bribery Convention establishes legally binding standards to criminalize bribery of foreign public officials in international business transactions. Five nonmember countries have adopted the OECD convention: Argentina, Brazil, Bulgaria, Russia, and South Africa.

[17]The UN Convention against Corruption calls for participating countries to criminalize acts of corruption and to agree to cooperate with one another to fight against and prevent corruption. Angola, Ghana, and Kenya, our case-study countries, are also signatories to this convention.

[18]Transparency International's 2011 Bribe Payers Index ranks 28 of the world's largest economies according to the perceived likelihood that companies from these countries would pay bribes abroad, based on the views of business executives as captured by Transparency International's 2011 Bribe Payers Survey. In the index, lower rankings indicate lower perceived likelihood of paying bribes abroad. The index ranks only Russian firms higher than Chinese firms.

U.S. and Chinese Government Agencies Engaged in Sub-Saharan Africa

U.S. Government Entities

Multiple U.S. agencies oversee and implement U.S. aid, trade, and investment activities in sub-Saharan Africa. Table 1 lists selected U.S. government entities' roles and responsibilities and areas of involvement.

Table 1: Selected U.S. Government Entities' Roles and Areas of Involvement in Sub-Saharan Africa

U.S. government entity	Roles and responsibilities	Area(s) of involvement
Department of State (State)	Oversees policy development and bilateral relations; provides diplomatic presence supporting U.S. aid, trade, investment activities; supports Commerce's commercial diplomacy activities, especially where Commerce is not present.	Trade, aid, investment
Department of Commerce (Commerce)	Provides Commercial Service presence and supports trade missions to facilitate U.S. export and investment opportunities; helps U.S. firms resolve market-access problems and address trade-agreement compliance issues; assists U.S. firms competing for foreign-government contracts through its Advocacy Center.	Trade, investment
Department of the Treasury (Treasury)	Advocates for improvements to regulatory frameworks, transparency, and governance through multilateral development banks, such as the World Bank, to enhance private-sector investment; provides bilateral technical assistance in areas such as budget and economic policy.	Aid, investment
Office of the U.S. Trade Representative (USTR)	Develops and coordinates implementation of U.S. trade and investment policy, including trade preferences; leads discussions with Trade and Investment Framework Agreement partners; negotiates bilateral investment treaties and other trade agreements.	Trade, investment
U.S. Agency for International Development (USADI)	Formulates U.S. development policies; implements U.S. development assistance activities through grants.	Aid
Millennium Challenge Corporation (MCC)	Implements bilateral compacts for grant-funded development projects, including infrastructure construction; has signed compacts with 13 sub-Saharan African countries.	Aid
Export-Import Bank of the United States (U.S. Ex-Im)	Provides financing—such as working capital guarantees (preexport financing), export credit insurance, loan guarantees, and direct loans (mostly nonconcessional)—to promote U.S. exports.	Trade
Overseas Private Investment Corporation (OPIC)	Assists U.S. private sector investors overseas through direct loans, loan guarantees, political risk insurance, and support for private equity investment funds.	Investment
U.S. Trade and Development Agency	Funds project-planning activities, such as feasibility studies, and U.S. visits for African entrepreneurs to facilitate exports of U.S. goods. and services	Trade, investment

Source: GAO analysis of information from State, Commerce, Treasury, USTR, USAID, MCC, U.S. Ex-Im, OPIC, and the U.S. Trade and Development Agency.

| Chinese Government Entities | China's Ministry of Commerce formulates and implements policies for foreign trade, economic cooperation, and overseas investments, in collaboration with other agencies.[19] The Ministry of Commerce also leads China's foreign aid by selecting projects and organizing the implementation of aid activities. Table 2 lists selected Chinese government entities' roles and responsibilities and areas of involvement. |

Table 2: Selected Chinese Government Entities' Roles and Areas of Involvement in Sub-Saharan Africa

Chinese government entity	Roles and responsibilities	Areas of involvement
Ministry of Commerce	Formulates and implements policies on foreign trade and investment activities; leads foreign aid efforts.	Trade, aid, investment
Ministry of Finance	Supervises and audits implementation of foreign aid budget.	Aid
Ministry of Foreign Affairs	Coordinates with other Chinese ministries on issues including foreign trade and economic cooperation and assistance.	Trade, aid, investment
Export-Import Bank of China (China Ex-Im)	Supports Chinese government policy to promote Chinese exports and investment through export credits, international guarantees, concessional and nonconcessional loans for overseas construction and investment, and official lines of credit.	Trade, aid, investment
China Development Bank	Serves Chinese government's policy to promote trade and investment by providing large-scale, long-term funding for construction of infrastructure and industrial projects; oversees China-Africa Development Fund, which encourages Chinese investments in Africa.	Trade, investment

Source: GAO analysis of information from the Brookings Institution, the Center for Global Development, the government of China, the World Bank, and China scholar Deborah Brautigam.

Note: Although China does not have an official aid agency, China's Ministries of Commerce, Finance, and Foreign Affairs and the Export-Import Bank of China are among the entities involved in China's development assistance activities.

According to a white paper issued by the Chinese government, the Ministry of Commerce is authorized to oversee foreign aid.[20] In addition, China's Ministry of Finance manages the budget for foreign aid expenditures, in cooperation with the Ministry of Commerce. The Ministry

[19]For example, China's State-owned Assets Supervision and Administration Commission of the State Council supervises and manages state-owned enterprises, and oversees related outbound investment.

[20]The white paper was published on the Chinese state-run news agency's website. See Information Office of the State Council, People's Republic of China, "White Paper: China's Foreign Aid" (April 2011), accessed Oct. 17, 2011, http://news.xinhuanet.com/english2010/china/2011-04/21/c_13839683.htm.

of Foreign Affairs manages China's diplomatic presence and drafts annual aid plans with the Ministry of Commerce.[21]

China Ex-Im and the China Development Bank, two of the Chinese government's financing institutions, promote the government's goals overseas. China Ex-Im maintains sole responsibility for concessional loans to support China's exports to sub-Saharan Africa and promotes Chinese exports and investment through export credits, international guarantees, and concessional and nonconcessional loans for overseas construction and investment. The China Development Bank provides large-scale, long-term funding for infrastructure construction and industrial projects; provides market-rate (nonconcessional) loans; and oversees the China-Africa Development Fund, to encourage Chinese investments throughout Africa.

U.S. Goals Have Emphasized Democracy and Development in Sub-Saharan Africa, while China's Policy Underscores Mutual Benefit and Noninterference

The United States' key priorities in sub-Saharan Africa include, among others, building democracy, promoting development, supporting commerce, and strengthening security. Also, in 2000, Congress passed the African Growth and Opportunity Act (AGOA), which extended trade preferences to eligible countries in the region.[22] The Chinese government has published policy papers that articulate its goal of establishing closer ties with African countries and state its principles of engagement, which include seeking mutual benefit for China and African nations and not interfering in African countries' domestic affairs.

---

[21]According to scholar Deborah Brautigam, China's Ministries of Commerce and Foreign Affairs have an uneasy division of labor and sharing of authorities over foreign aid. See Deborah Brautigam, *The Dragon's Gift: The Real Story of China in Africa* (New York, N.Y.: Oxford University Press, 2009), 111.

[22]Pub. L. No. 106-200, as amended (codified at 19 U.S.C. §§ 3701 *et seq*).

U.S. Goals and Programs for Sub-Saharan Africa Include Focus on Development and Emphasis on Democracy and Economic Growth

The U.S. government has articulated its goals for sub-Saharan Africa through annual Department of State (State) bureau plans for the region and through a U.S. strategy announced in June 2012. The fiscal year 2013 State bureau plan for sub-Saharan Africa identifies a number of goals, including strengthening democratic institutions, building respect for human rights, ensuring countries are free of conflict, using U.S. development assistance to improve health and education indicators, and helping sub-Saharan African countries build their share of global trade.[23] According to State officials, State's annual bureau plan had served as the primary U.S. strategy for the region. However, in June 2012, the U.S. government publicly issued its interagency "U.S. Strategy Toward Sub-Saharan Africa."[24] In his letter introducing the current strategy, President Obama highlighted goals related to strengthening democratic institutions and growing Africa's economy as priority efforts critical to the region. The 2012 U.S. strategy articulates four objectives for U.S. interaction with the region that are consistent with the goals in State's bureau plan: strengthen democratic institutions; spur economic growth, trade, and investment; advance peace and security; and promote opportunity and development.

According to U.S. officials, the 2012 strategy is intended to encourage an interagency approach for engagement with sub-Saharan Africa, with greater emphasis on economic and commercial activities.[25] State, Commerce, USAID, and USTR officials said that several agencies are developing plans to coordinate in implementing the strategy's four objectives. Furthermore, according to a State document, U.S. agencies are working to better link trade policy and development objectives. In addition, State has issued a directive to prioritize economic issues in U.S. foreign policy worldwide, including efforts to improve regional economic integration and introduce U.S. businesses to new markets in sub-Saharan

---

[23]State's fiscal year 2013 bureau plan for sub-Saharan Africa identified additional goals related to adapting to climate change, enhancing food security and sustainable agricultural development, building public support for a mutually beneficial U.S.-Africa partnership, and increasing U.S. diplomatic effectiveness.

[24]White House, "U.S. Strategy Toward Sub-Saharan Africa" (June 2012), accessed June 14, 2012, http://www.whitehouse.gov/sites/default/files/docs/africa_strategy_2.pdf.

[25]Commerce officials noted that, pursuant to the 2012 strategy, Commerce is leading the development of an initiative called "Doing Business in Africa" that combines the tools of U.S. trade promotion agencies to assist U.S. firms in exploring commercial opportunities in sub-Saharan Africa.

Africa. In October 2011, Secretary of State Hillary Clinton stated that, as part of this effort, the U.S. government is evolving its development efforts throughout Africa to increase investments and reinforce, but not replace, what these markets can achieve independently. The President's 2011 Trade Policy Agenda, coordinated by USTR, also states an interest in expanding markets for U.S. goods and services in sub-Saharan Africa and building the region's economic development through trade.[26]

Increased trade with sub-Saharan Africa was identified as a primary U.S. goal in the African Growth and Opportunity Act (AGOA), which was signed into law in 2000 to promote stable and sustainable economic growth and development in the region. AGOA allows eligible sub-Saharan African countries[27] to export to the United States, without import duties, qualifying goods from a list of more than 6,000 items.[28] Currently, 39 countries are eligible for AGOA benefits. As part of AGOA's "third-country fabric provision," a subset of those countries can export to the United States, subject to a cap, apparel made with yarns and fabrics originating anywhere in the world.[29] AGOA also called for an annual forum, known as the U.S.–Sub-Saharan Africa Trade and Economic Forum—a high-level economic dialogue among U.S. and African senior government officials, members of their respective private sectors, and representatives of civil society. U.S. officials have described the annual forum, which has been

---

[26] Office of the United States Trade Representative, "2011 Trade Policy Agenda and 2010 Annual Report," accessed January 12, 2012, http://www.ustr.gov/webfm_send/2597.

[27] AGOA authorizes the President to designate countries as eligible to receive AGOA benefits if they are determined to have established, or are making continual progress toward establishing, the following: market-based economies; the rule of law and political pluralism; elimination of barriers to U.S. trade and investment; protection of intellectual property; efforts to combat corruption; policies to reduce poverty and increase availability of health care and educational opportunities; protection of human rights and worker rights; and elimination of certain child labor practices.

[28] The United States also offers tariff reductions for goods from most sub-Saharan African countries under the Generalized System of Preferences (GSP). The Africa Investment Incentive Act of 2006, Pub. L. No. 109-432, div. D, Title VI, expanded the list of products that eligible sub-Saharan African countries may export to the United States duty free under GSP, which covers approximately 4,600 items. GSP and AGOA eligibility criteria overlap, and countries must be GSP eligible to take advantage of trade benefits under AGOA.

[29] This subset includes "lesser developed beneficiary countries" as defined by AGOA, which include countries, such as Ghana and Kenya, that the UN does not classify as least developed countries. In August 2012, Congress voted to extend the third-country fabric provision, which was set to expire the following month. See Pub. L. No. 112-163.

held in Washington, D.C., and various locations in Africa, as a way to link trade capacity building and trade opportunities. The U.S. government released the "U.S. Strategy Toward Sub-Saharan Africa" at the 2012 forum, which was held in Washington, D.C., and focused on sub-Saharan Africa's infrastructure development to promote trade among the countries of the region and with the United States.

The U.S. government also established trade and investment agreements with sub-Saharan African countries and regional economic communities to promote cooperation on trade and investment issues, including strengthening bilateral ties, improving the business environment, and building trade capacity.[30] These agreements include bilateral investment treaties, which establish some protections and regulations for U.S. investments in partner countries.[31]

In addition, the U.S. government maintains a number of development assistance programs in sub-Saharan Africa to help meet stated goals on promoting opportunity and development.[32] These programs include the Global Health Initiative, which integrates U.S.-funded global health efforts such as HIV/AIDS and malaria; Feed the Future, the U.S. government-wide strategy to address global hunger and food security; the Global Climate Change Initiative, which is intended to better integrate climate-change considerations into U.S. foreign assistance; Millennium Challenge Corporation (MCC) compacts and other programs, which provide grants

---

[30]For example, the U.S. government has Trade and Investment Framework Agreements in sub-Saharan Africa with Angola, Ghana, Liberia, Mauritius, Mozambique, Nigeria, Rwanda, and South Africa as well as with the Common Market for Eastern and Southern Africa, the East African Community, and the West African Economic and Monetary Union. The U.S. government also has a Trade, Investment, and Development Cooperative Agreement with the Southern African Customs Union. In addition, according to Commerce officials, the U.S. Department of Commerce recently established the U.S.–East African Community Commercial Dialogue, the first such effort in Africa, to enable the United States and East African Community governments to work with their respective private sectors to increase two-way trade and investment.

[31]The U.S. government has bilateral investment treaties with Cameroon, the Democratic Republic of the Congo, Mozambique, the Republic of the Congo, Rwanda, and Senegal.

[32]In addition to providing bilateral assistance to countries in sub-Saharan Africa, the United States assists the region through its membership in, and contributions to, multilateral organizations. According to U.S. officials, the U.S. government's position as the largest shareholder at the World Bank and the largest nonregional shareholder at the African Development Bank enables it to advance U.S. priorities in sub-Saharan Africa through these institutions.

for development projects to eligible countries; and Partnership for Growth, a U.S. partnership with select countries to promote economic growth through country ownership and joint decision making. [33]

China's Stated Policy for Africa Emphasizes Mutual Benefit and Noninterference

The Chinese government's policies and goals toward sub-Saharan Africa, while not specifically defined for the region, are reflected in two publicly released documents—its African Policy, issued in 2006, [34] and its policy on foreign aid, issued in 2011. [35] The 2006 African Policy states that China's objective in Africa is to promote long-term China-Africa relations in a mutually beneficial manner. The 2006 policy document outlines an approach that includes the principles of respecting African countries' independence and equality; seeking mutual benefit in economic development and cooperation on social development; fostering cooperation with Africa in the United Nations and other multilateral systems; and enhancing mutual learning in areas such as governance and development. Additionally, the 2006 document states that to establish relations with China, a country must adhere to the "one China" principle—that is, cease official relations with Taiwan. [36]

Regarding trade relations with Africa, China's 2006 African Policy includes plans to facilitate access for African commodities to the Chinese market and provide duty-free treatment for imports of some goods from least developed countries, including those in Africa. Additionally, the 2006 policy document expresses support for Chinese investments in Africa and

---

[33]In sub-Saharan Africa, Ghana and Tanzania participate in the Partnership for Growth Initiative.

[34]Ministry of Foreign Affairs, People's Republic of China, "China's African Policy," accessed October 11, 2011, http://www.fmprc.gov.cn/eng/zxxx/t230615.htm.

[35]The policy is stated in a white paper published on the Chinese state-run news agency's website. See Information Office of the State Council, People's Republic of China, "White Paper: China's Foreign Aid," accessed October 11, 2011, http://news.xinhuanet.com/english2010/china/2011-04/21/c_13839683.htm.

[36]This report did not include an analysis of U.S. or Chinese security-related goals in sub-Saharan Africa. We did not obtain information on China's security goals or policies in the region.

announces continued assistance for Chinese firms through loans and credit lines with preferential terms.[37]

China's published policy on foreign aid, released in 2011, specifies goals that include helping recipient countries, including those in Africa, build development capacity, improve livelihoods, and promote economic growth and social progress. The 2011 policy document emphasizes "South-South cooperation" on foreign aid, indicating that China views itself as a developing country mutually engaged with other developing countries. Similar in content to China's African Policy, the 2011 policy document notes the following principles of China's foreign aid policy:

- helping countries build their own capacity for development and self-reliance by fostering local personnel and technical capacity, building infrastructure, and using domestic resources;
- not imposing political conditions or interfering in countries' internal affairs, and respecting recipient countries' role in guiding their own development;
- fostering equality and mutual benefit and accommodating recipient countries' interests;
- maintaining a realistic sense of China's capacity and resources to provide assistance, while recognizing the needs of recipient countries; and
- attending to reform and innovation to improve the outcomes of foreign aid.

China's 2011 policy document also indicates that China provides resources for foreign aid through grants, and interest-free and concessional loans. China offers foreign aid in the form of projects, goods and materials, emergency aid, and debt relief, among others. Moreover, the 2011 document states that 40 percent of China's global foreign aid expenditures in recipient countries worldwide are for construction projects in which China provides some or all of the financing, services, materials, and labor. Unlike the United States and other nations, China is not a member of the OECD's Development Assistance Committee and has not agreed to eliminate the tying of aid to the use of its own goods and

---

[37]China's trade activities in Africa are also partly driven by its "Going Global" policy, initiated in 1999, which encouraged Chinese firms to seek trade and investment opportunities globally, and as part of which large, generally state-supported Chinese firms make investments to boost China's long-term national growth.

services.[38] However, U.S. officials said that China's participation in the Fourth High-Level Forum on Aid Effectiveness in Busan, South Korea, in November 2011, along with 100 other countries that also are not OECD members, reinforced support for the 2005 Paris Declaration on Aid Effectiveness and represented a significant recognition of China's role in development assistance. China's 2011 policy document states that Chinese experts working on construction projects will adopt the same standards of living as experts in the recipient country. In addition, China's 2006 African Policy states that the government supports continued financing for Chinese enterprises' investment and business engagement in Africa. Scholars and U.S. officials have also said that China actively uses its financing and assistance activities to facilitate opportunities for Chinese firms.

The Chinese government has also articulated aspects of its policy toward Africa, including sub-Saharan Africa, at the Forum on China-Africa Cooperation (FOCAC). The Chinese government initiated FOCAC in 2000 as a high-level platform to announce major Chinese initiatives, such as large infrastructure financing packages and trade preferences for Africa, and has convened high-level Chinese and African officials every 3 years since 2000. At the 2012 FOCAC, held in Beijing, the Chinese government reiterated principles from prior meetings and previously issued policy documents, including maintaining high-level engagement, strengthening China-Africa dialogue, and enhancing mutual trust. At that meeting, China also doubled its commitments for financing infrastructure and other development in Africa to $20 billion, from the $10 billion commitment that it announced in 2009; expanded duty-free treatment for certain African exports to China; and reiterated use of the China-Africa Development Fund, which was established in 2006 to fund up to $5 billion in Chinese firms' investments in Africa in sectors such as agriculture, infrastructure, and natural resources. According to an article from the Centre for Chinese Studies in South Africa, the South African president's critical statements about aspects of China's presence in Africa made at the 2012 FOCAC showed Africans taking a greater stake in shaping the

---

[38]China is a participant in the 2005 Paris Declaration on Aid Effectiveness, in which donor and partner countries agreed to improve aid effectiveness through results-oriented assistance and donor coordination, among other principles. However, U.S. officials noted that China had a nonbinding role in the Paris Declaration and therefore cannot be held accountable to other donors.

dialogue with China, in contrast to previous FOCAC sessions.[39] In addition, in a speech delivered before the start of the 2012 FOCAC, Chinese Premier Wen Jiabao spoke about unresolved issues in China's relationship with Africa, including the need to diversify trade and investments and increase technology transfer. Figure 2 presents a timeline of key FOCAC announcements in 2000 through 2012.

Figure 2: Key Chinese Government Announcements at the Forum on China-Africa Cooperation (FOCAC), 2000-2012

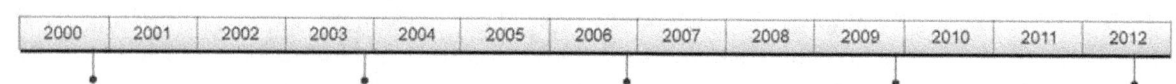

| 2000 | 2001 | 2002 | 2003 | 2004 | 2005 | 2006 | 2007 | 2008 | 2009 | 2010 | 2011 | 2012 |

Beijing, China (inaugural)
October 2000

- Outlined principles of cooperation including equality and mutual benefit and pursuit of common progress
- Pledged continued assistance through grants and concessional and interest-free loans
- Offered to set up funds to encourage Chinese investment
- Established fund to train African professionals in various disciplines
- Set up joint follow-up mechanisms to evaluate progress

Addis Ababa, Ethiopia
December 2003

- Announced duty-free treatment on some African exports from least developed countries
- Approved debt relief and debt cancellation for 31 African countries and cancelled 156 matured debts
- Resolved to increase cooperation and to continue peacekeeping efforts
- Proposed programs to promote cultural and diplomatic exchanges

Beijing, China
November 2006

Chinese government released African Policy in January

- Established China-Africa Development Fund of up to $5 billion to encourage Chinese investments in Africa
- Announced that development assistance would double by 2009, totaling $5 billion in preferential loans and export buyer's credits to African countries
- Pledged 100 Chinese experts and 10 demonstration centers for agricultural technology development
- Identified infrastructure development as key area of cooperation and pledged support for Chinese businesses working in this sector in Africa

Sharm El Sheikh, Egypt
November 2009

- Committed $10 billion in preferential loans by 2012, largely for infrastructure and social development
- Announced duty-free treatment for 60 percent of exports from least developed countries that have diplomatic relations with China by 2010, with goal of 95 percent in future
- Committed $1 billion in loans from Chinese financial institutions to develop small and medium-sized African enterprises
- Canceled interest-free government loans that matured by end of 2009 for heavily indebted poor countries and least developed countries
- Appointed Chinese government special representative for African affairs

Beijing, China
July 2012

- Pledged $20 billion credit line to African countries for infrastructure, agriculture, manufacturing, and small and medium-sized enterprises
- Announced duty-free treatment for 97 percent of tariff items from least developed countries that have diplomatic relations with China
- Identified plan for investment and trade promotion missions to Africa and for exhibitions of African exports to China
- Announced program to train 30,000 African professionals in various sectors and to offer 18,000 government scholarships
- Pledged to cooperate on clean energy and renewable resource projects, protect local environment, and promote sustainable development

Source: GAO analysis of Chinese government information.

---

[39]M. McDonald, "After FOCAC: Have China-Africa Relations Finally Turned a Corner, or Was FOCAC V Simply More of the Same?" *African East-Asian Affairs/China Monitor* (2012).

Data Show Growth in U.S. and Chinese Trade with Sub-Saharan Africa since 2001, but Data on China's Grants, Loans, and Investments Are Limited

Both U.S. and Chinese trade in goods with sub-Saharan Africa increased from 2001 through 2011, with Chinese trade increasing faster and surpassing U.S. trade in 2009. Imports of crude oil have dominated both countries' trade with sub-Saharan Africa. U.S. government aid in the form of grants increased from 2001 through 2010, and U.S. government loans to support U.S. exports and investments increased from 2001 through 2011; data on Chinese government grants and loans to sub-Saharan Africa are limited. Data for 2007 through 2011 suggest that U.S. foreign direct investment flows to the region were larger than China's.[40] Mining, including petroleum extraction, was the top investment sector in sub-Saharan Africa for both countries.[41]

U.S. and Chinese Trade in Goods with Sub-Saharan Africa Increased from 2001 to 2011

China overtook the United States as sub-Saharan Africa's largest trading partner in 2009. The United States' and China's total trade in goods with sub-Saharan Africa increased each year from 2001 through 2011, except in 2009 when total trade declined during the global economic crisis (see fig. 3).[42] During that year, China's trade declined by less than the United States', and China overtook the United States as sub-Saharan Africa's largest trading partner. For the United States, growth in imports accounted for 80 percent of growth in total trade from 2001 through 2011; for China, growth in imports accounted for 56 percent of growth in total trade for the same period. China's exports overtook U.S. exports in 2003, with the value of China's exports almost triple the level of U.S. exports in 2011.

---

[40]According to OECD, foreign direct investment is the ownership by a foreign person or business of 10 percent or more of the voting equity of a firm located in the host country. Foreign direct investment flows provide information for foreign direct investment activity within a given *period* of time, while foreign direct investment stock indicates the level of foreign direct investment at a given *point* in time.

[41]Petroleum includes oil (crude and refined) and petroleum products (e.g., jelly and waxes).

[42]Total trade in goods is defined as imports plus exports. In 2011, trade with the United States and China represented an estimated 31 percent of sub-Saharan Africa's total trade, while sub-Saharan Africa represented 3 percent of total trade for both the United States and China.

Figure 3: U.S. and Chinese Total Trade, Imports, and Exports of Goods to Sub-Saharan Africa, 2001-2011

Dollars in billions

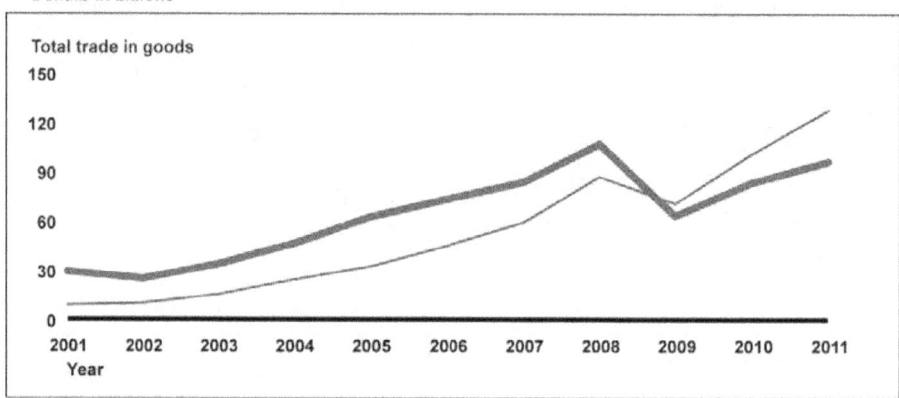

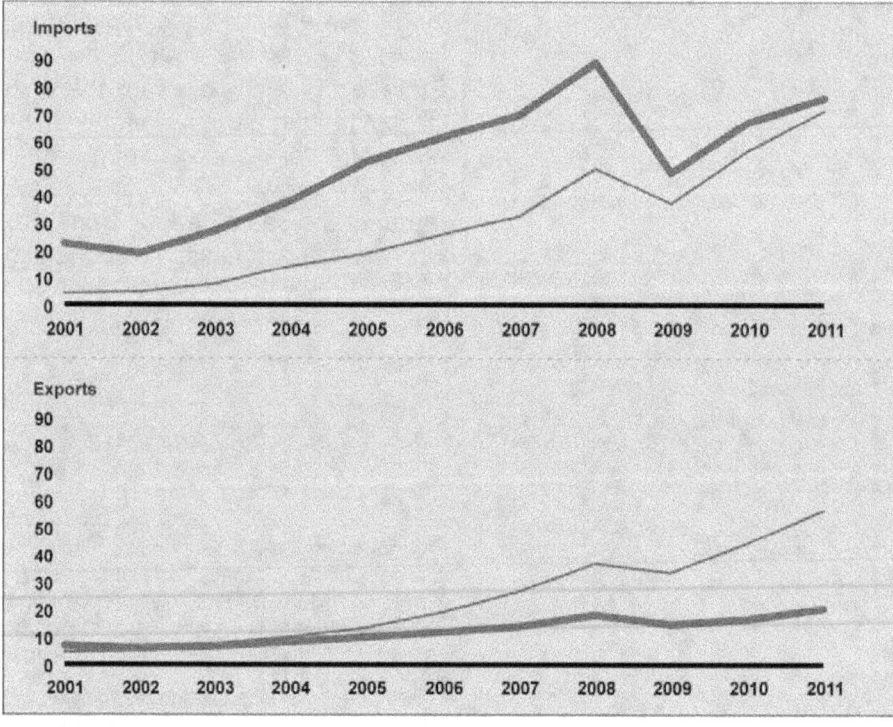

Source: GAO analysis of UN data.

GAO-13-199 Sub-Saharan Africa

Crude Oil and Other Natural Resources Have Dominated U.S. and Chinese Imports of Goods from Sub-Saharan Africa

Natural resources have constituted the bulk of U.S. and Chinese imports from sub-Saharan Africa. In 2011, petroleum and petroleum products, primarily crude oil, accounted for 81 percent of the value of U.S. imports, while ores, metals, and minerals accounted for 9 percent. By comparison, petroleum and petroleum products, almost exclusively crude oil, accounted for 59 percent of the value of Chinese imports, while ores, metals, and minerals accounted for 32 percent.[43] As figure 4 shows, U.S. and Chinese imports of petroleum and petroleum products, as well as Chinese imports of ores, metals, and minerals, from sub-Saharan Africa have increased since 2001.[44]

---

[43]Examples of U.S. imports of ores, metals, and minerals are platinum and diamonds. Examples of Chinese imports of ores, metals, and minerals include iron ore and copper.

[44]For example, in 2001, 68 percent of U.S. imports of goods from sub-Saharan Africa were petroleum and petroleum products and 14 percent were ores, metals, and minerals. In 2001, 61 percent of Chinese imports were petroleum and petroleum products and 19 percent was ores, metals, and minerals.

Figure 4: U.S. and Chinese Imports of Goods from Sub-Saharan Africa, 2001-2011

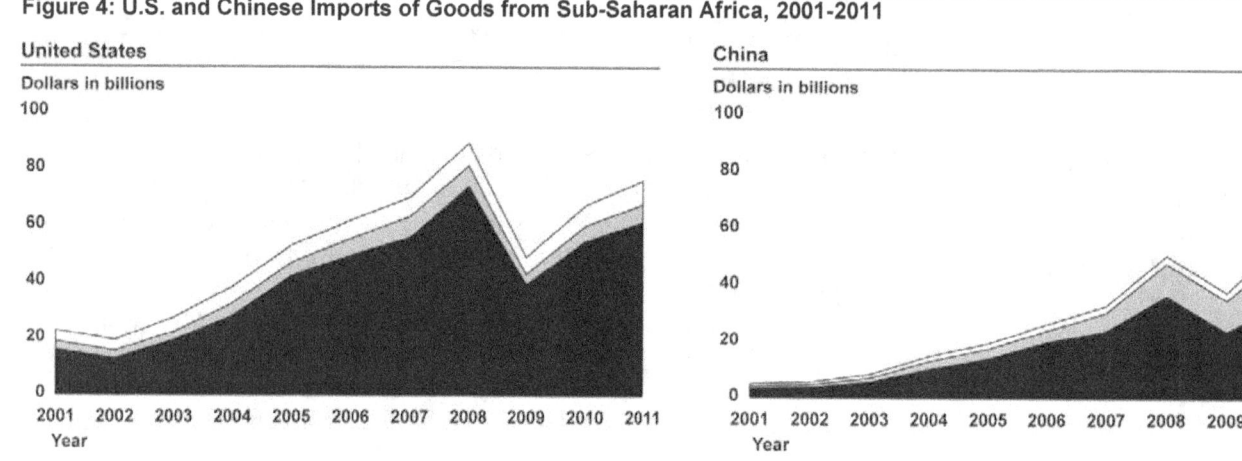

Source: GAO analysis of UN data.

Notes: Import values are shown in nominal dollars. Data for Chinese imports have been adjusted to exclude imports of a category of goods labeled "special transactions," for consistency with data reported by the IMF's Direction of Trade Statistics and the World Trade Atlas.

The majority of U.S. imports from sub-Saharan Africa enter the United States without tariffs under AGOA. In 2011, imports under AGOA were approximately 70 percent of the total value of U.S. imports from sub-Saharan Africa.[45] Petroleum imports, primarily from Nigeria and to a lesser extent from Angola, constituted almost 92 percent of AGOA imports, while two categories of goods—transportation equipment and textiles, apparel, leather and footwear—were the primary nonpetroleum AGOA imports (see fig. 5).[46]

[45]In 2011, an additional 3 percent received duty-free treatment under GSP. According to USTR, goods from certain countries can also enter duty free under other U.S. trade provisions.

[46]Transportation equipment represented nearly 4 percent, and textiles, apparel, leather, and footwear represented nearly 2 percent of imports under AGOA in 2011. From 2001 to 2011, the value of nonpetroleum U.S. imports under AGOA increased 322 percent, from about $1 billion to $4.3 billion.

Figure 5: U.S. Imports of Goods from Sub-Saharan Africa under AGOA, 2001-2011

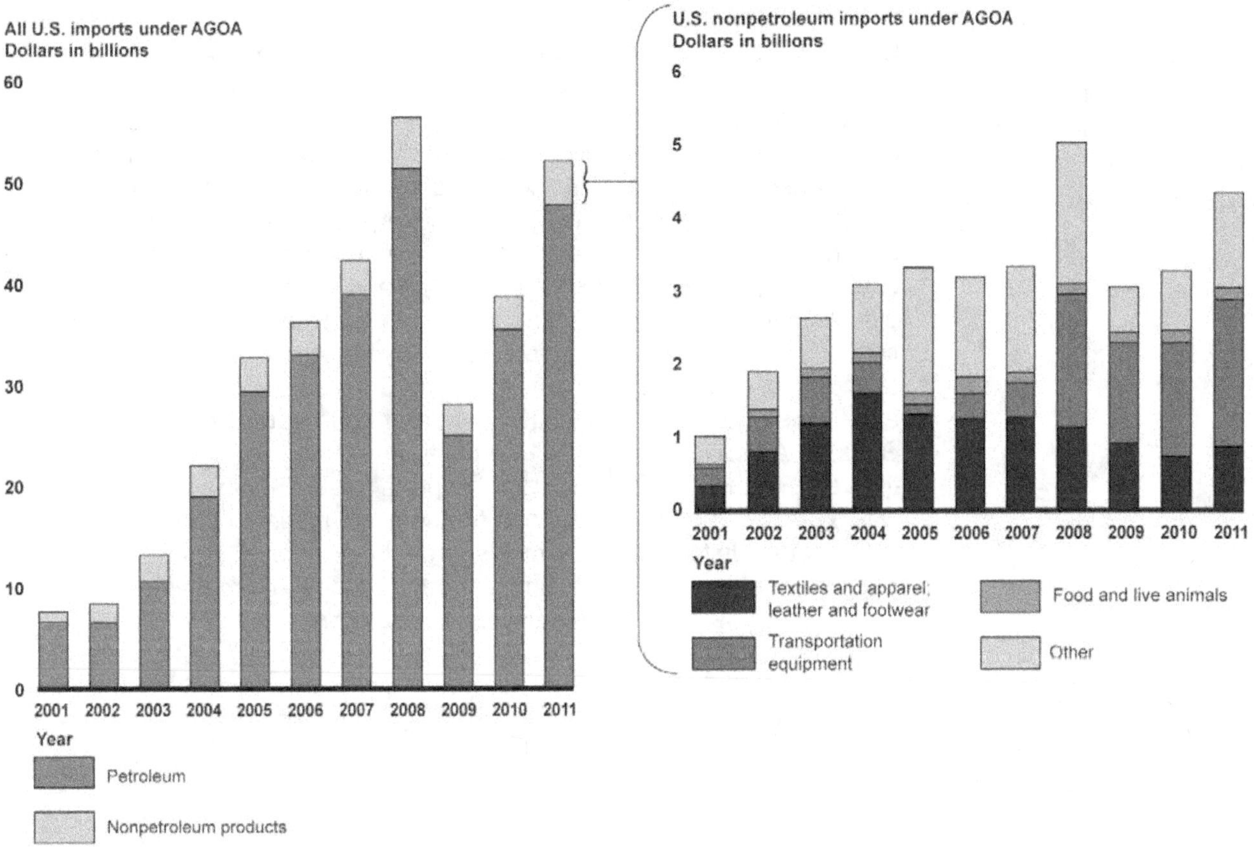

All U.S. imports under AGOA
Dollars in billions

U.S. nonpetroleum imports under AGOA
Dollars in billions

Source: GAO analysis of Department of Commerce data.

Note: Import values are shown in nominal dollars.

Almost all Chinese imports from least developed countries in Africa enter China without tariffs.[47] In 2003, China announced that some commodities from least developed countries in Africa would be given duty-free status. By 2007, according to a report by the World Trade Organization that cited Chinese officials, 98 percent of the total value of Chinese imports from

---

[47]In contrast to the list of sub-Saharan African countries eligible for AGOA trade preferences, China's list of eligible countries includes only least developed countries. For example, in 2012, 40 sub-Saharan African countries were eligible for AGOA while 30 sub-Saharan African countries were eligible for China's trade preferences.

least developed countries, including sub-Saharan African countries, was exported to China duty free.[48]

Chinese Exports of Machinery, Transport Equipment, and Manufactured Goods Exceeded U.S. Exports of Goods to Sub-Saharan Africa

Chinese exports to sub-Saharan Africa increased more rapidly than U.S. exports from 2001 through 2011. The value of U.S. exports tripled during this period, from $6.8 billion to $20.3 billion, while the value of Chinese exports grew by a factor of nearly 13, from $4.4 billion to $56.3 billion. The largest category of U.S. exports to sub-Saharan Africa by value was machinery and transport equipment; the largest categories of Chinese exports were manufactured goods and machinery and transport equipment (see fig. 6). The United States and China generally exported different types of machinery and transport equipment: motor vehicles and civil-engineering equipment were key U.S. exports, while ships and telecommunications equipment were key Chinese exports. In 2011, U.S. and Chinese exports of machinery and transport equipment to sub-Saharan Africa represented 41 percent and 40 percent, respectively, of the value of the two countries' total exports to sub-Saharan Africa, with China's exports of machinery and transport equipment almost triple the value of the United States'. China's largest category of exports was manufactured goods—for example, cotton fabrics and footwear—representing 49 percent of the value of its exports.

---

[48]See World Trade Organization, Trade Policy Review Body, *Trade Policy Review: Report by the Secretariat—China*, WT/TPR/S/199 (2008).

Figure 6: U.S. and Chinese Exports of Goods to Sub-Saharan Africa, 2001-2011

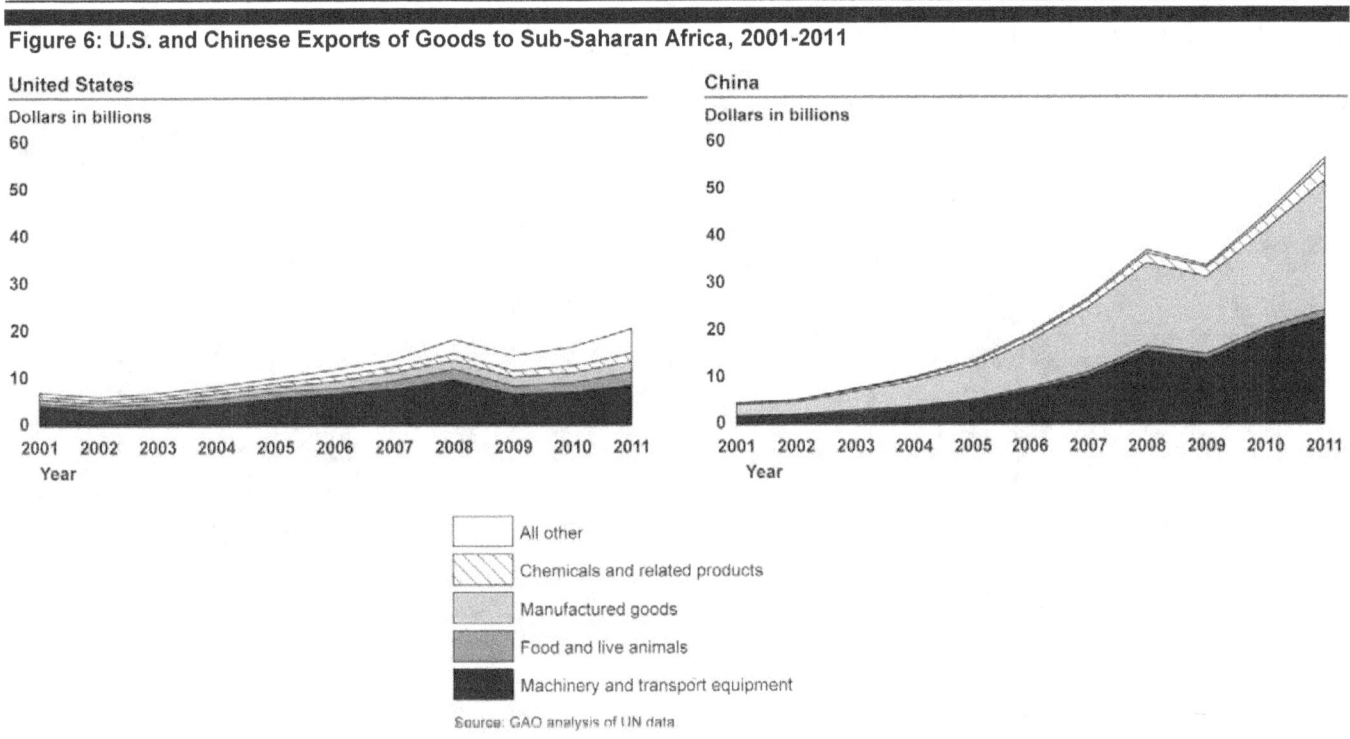

Source: GAO analysis of UN data.

Note: Export values are shown in nominal dollars.

United States and China Have Several Common Trading Partners in Sub-Saharan Africa, but China's Reach Is Greater

In 2011, the United States imported more than $1 billion in goods from each of eight sub-Saharan African countries, and China imported more than $1 billion in goods from each of nine countries. The United States and China each imported more than $1 billion in goods from Nigeria, Angola, South Africa, the Republic of the Congo, and Equatorial Guinea. The United States also imported more than $1 billion in goods from Gabon, Chad, and Côte d'Ivoire, while China imported more than $1 billion in goods from the Democratic Republic of the Congo, Zambia, Sudan, and Mauritania.[49]

---

[49]South Africa is sub-Saharan Africa's largest economy and represented 13 percent of U.S. imports in goods from sub-Saharan Africa and 23 percent of China's imports in 2011.

Figure 7: U.S. and Chinese Imports of Goods from Sub-Saharan Africa, by Value of Imports and Country of Origin, 2011

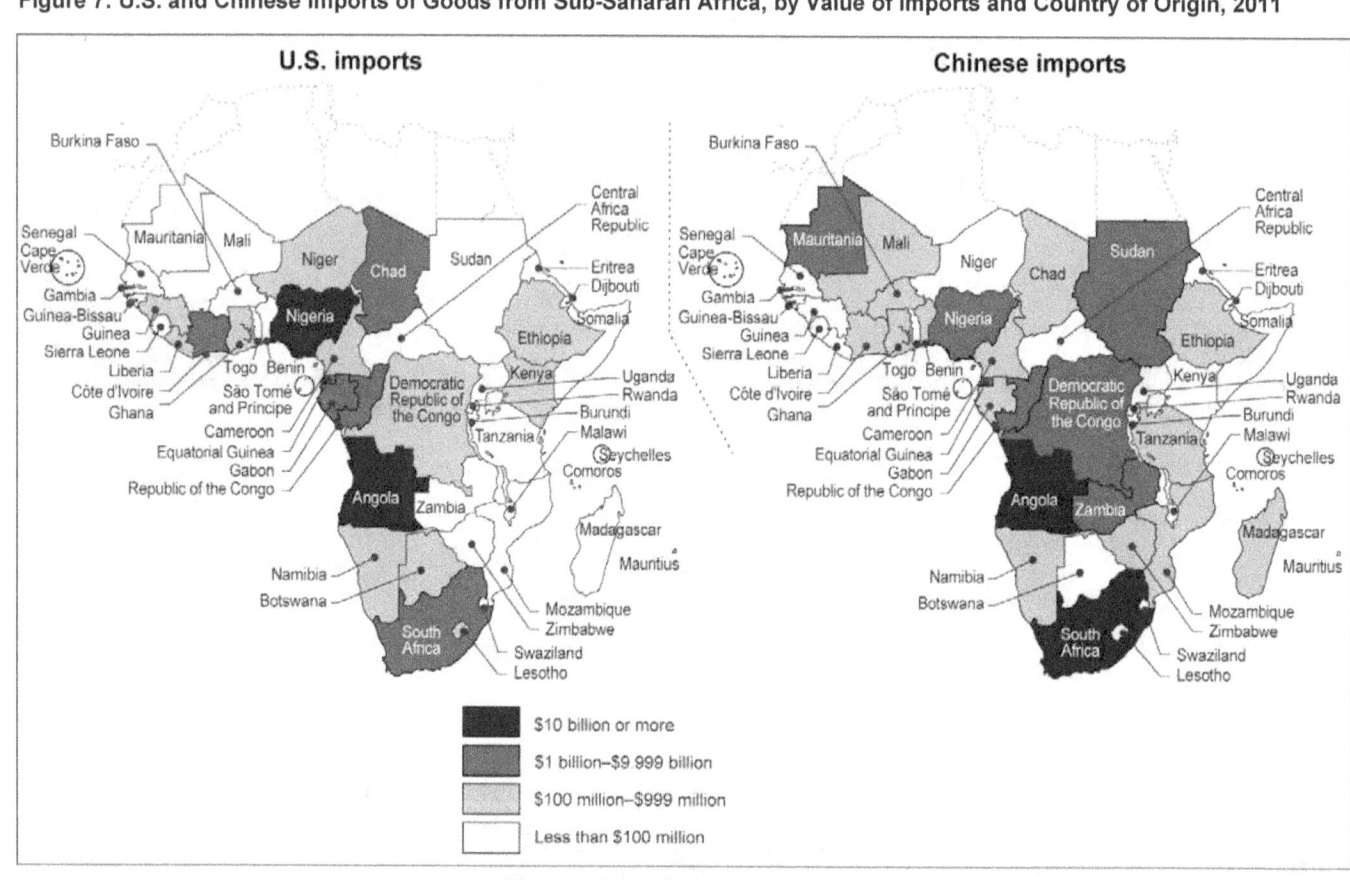

Source: GAO analysis of UN data; Map Resources (map).

With respect to exports, the United States exported more than $1 billion in goods to each of 4 countries in sub-Saharan Africa in 2011, whereas China exported at a similar level to 10 countries (see fig. 8). Both countries exported more than $1 billion in goods to South Africa, Nigeria, Angola, and Ghana.[50] In addition, China exported more than $1 billion in goods to Benin, Kenya, Tanzania, Togo, Liberia, and Sudan.

[50]South Africa received 34 percent of U.S. exports of goods to sub-Saharan Africa and 24 percent of Chinese exports to the region in 2011.

Figure 8: U.S. and Chinese Exports of Goods to Sub-Saharan Africa, by Value of Exports and Destination, 2011

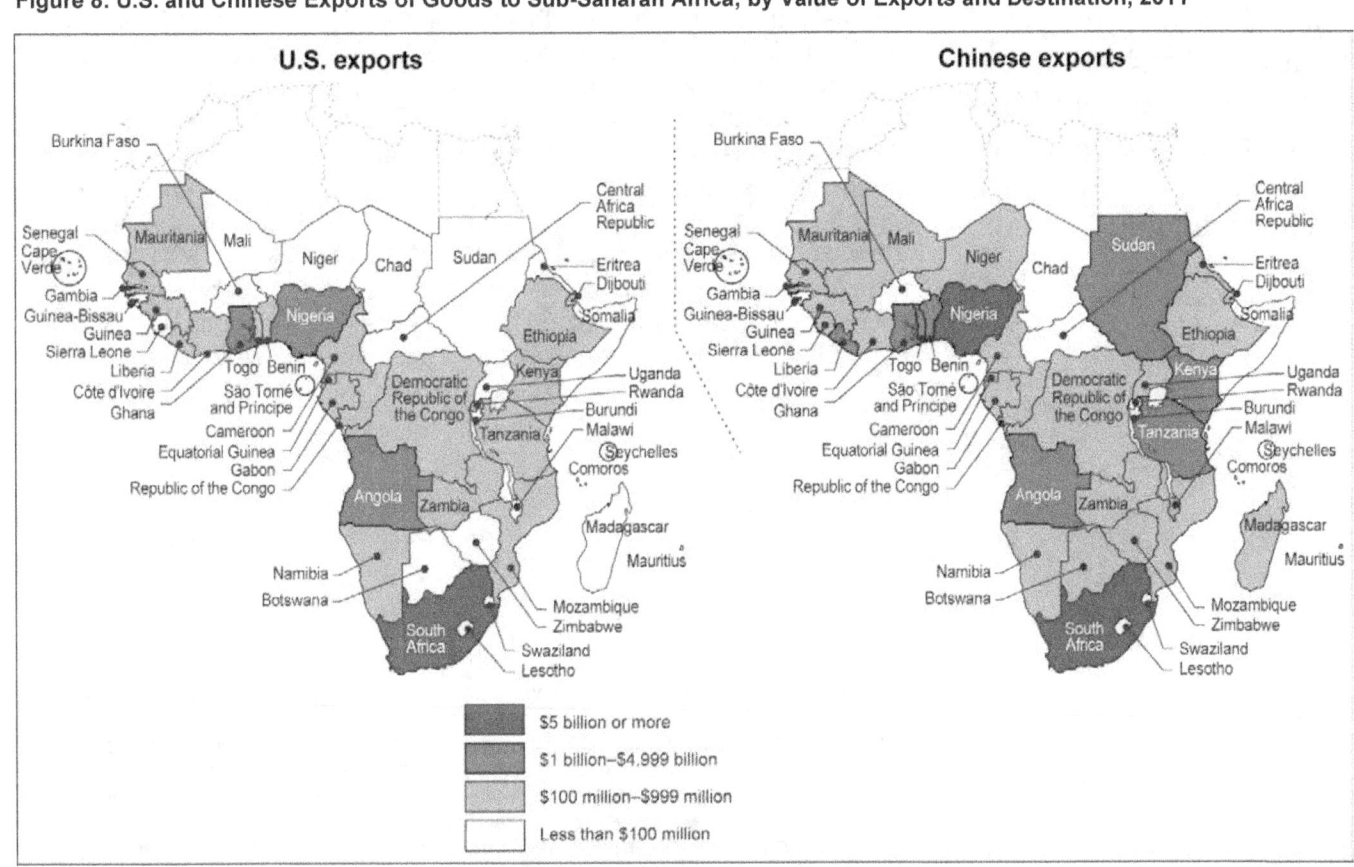

Source: GAO analysis of UN data; Map Resources (map).

U.S. Trade in Services with Sub-Saharan Africa Is Estimated to Exceed $11 Billion per Year, but Data on China's Trade in Services with the Region Are Unavailable

Estimates on U.S. trade in services indicate that the United States had a surplus in trade in services with sub-Saharan Africa from 2006 through 2011.[51] U.S. imports of services, excluding travel and passenger fares, averaged about $2.6 billion per year, and U.S. exports of services averaged about $9.1 billion per year.[52] The largest service sectors for U.S. imports were business, professional, and technical services; travel and passenger fares; and financial services. The largest service sectors for U.S. exports were business, professional, and technical services and travel and passenger fares.[53] Illustrating that business, professional, and technical services was a top sector for U.S. exports of services, data on contracts financed by the World Bank in sub-Saharan Africa from 2001 through 2011 show that most of U.S. firms' contracts were for consulting

---

[51]Trade in services refers to the buying and selling of intangible products and activities; examples of trade-in-services sectors include tourism, financial services, and telecommunications. Contracted activities, such as construction and consulting services, are also examples of trade-in-services activities. United States does not publish trade-in-services data for sub-Saharan Africa. However, BEA provided underlying tabulations from BEA and other sources that we used to estimate U.S. trade in services with sub-Saharan Africa. When BEA provided ranges of estimates for sectors of services such as business, professional, and technical services, we used the higher values to calculate estimates of total trade in services, including imports and exports of services. Therefore, the averages we report represent the higher values in underlying tabulations from BEA and other sources and our analysis of BEA's survey data. See appendix I for examples of these other sources.

[52]Our estimate of U.S. imports of services from sub-Saharan Africa does not include imports of travel and passenger fares, because regional sub-Saharan Africa data were not available for this category. However, U.S. imports of travel and passenger fares averaged $3.2 billion per year for 2006 through 2011 for all of Africa and averaged $1.2 billion for Angola, Ghana, and South Africa.

[53]From 2006 through 2011, annual U.S. imports averaged at least $1 billion for business, professional, and technical services; at least $1.2 billion for travel and passenger fares; and $250 million to $400 million for financial services. Because data on U.S. imports of travel and passenger fares were unavailable for sub-Saharan Africa, the $1.2 billion includes only data for Angola, Ghana, and South Africa as a minimum level of U.S. imports for travel and passenger fares. During the same period, annual U.S. exports averaged at least $2.7 billion for business, professional, and technical services and $1.7 billion for travel and passenger fares.

services and that these services accounted for 72 percent of the combined value of the U.S. firms' contracts.[54]

We were unable to obtain comparable data for China's trade in services with sub-Saharan Africa, in part because China does not publish regional or country-specific data.[55] However, according to experts and U.S. officials, China has been active in providing construction services. In addition, the data on World Bank–financed contracts show that most of Chinese firms' contracts were for construction services and that these services accounted for 91 percent of the combined value of the Chinese firms' contracts.[56] Figure 9 illustrates the data on World Bank–financed contracts with firms from the United States, China, and other countries in sub-Saharan Africa.

---

[54]Services provided by U.S. firms under World Bank–funded contracts represent a small fraction (less than 1 percent) of annual U.S. trade in service exports to sub-Saharan Africa. However, World Bank contracts represent one of the few instances in which data are available for examination of potential competition between U.S. and Chinese firms. According to the World Bank, the contract data include only contracts reviewed by World Bank staff prior to award, which constitute about 40 percent of total World Bank investment lending. In addition, the nationality of a firm reflects the country in which it is registered, although the firm's parent may be headquartered in another country.

[55]China's Ministry of Commerce publishes data on trade in services and also provides data on trade in services to the UN Service Trade database. These data include exports and imports globally and by sector but not by country. The Ministry of Commerce's data also include the number of Chinese workers abroad for all of Africa, Angola, Nigeria, and Sudan, providing an indicator of the magnitude of service exports to Africa and these countries (see supplemental report GAO-13-280SP for a discussion of the number of Chinese workers in Angola). The United States does not publish comparable data for American workers abroad.

[56]Construction contracts represented 55 percent and consulting contracts represented 21 percent of the total value of World Bank contracts for sub-Saharan Africa.

Figure 9: World Bank–Financed Contracts Won by Firms from the United States, China, and Other Countries in Sub-Saharan Africa, 2001-2011

Firm's country of origin	Number of contracts	World Bank contract dollars won, percentage	Contract value by categories, dollars in millions	Top three contract types, number of contracts
United States	631	1	$230 $16 $72	Management/technical advice .... 224 Feasibility studies .... 54 Sector studies 41
China	324	15	$3 $3,186 $307	Construction services, maintenance ...... 106 and rehabilitation Construction services, infrastructure .... 79 Equipment, electricial 32
Other countries[a]	22,345	84	$4,614 $10,066 $5,443	Management/technical advice .... 3,403 Project management .... 1,557 Construction services, maintenance and rehabilitation 1,506

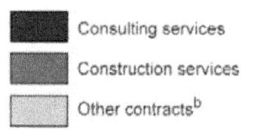

■ Consulting services

▨ Construction services

☐ Other contracts[b]

Source: GAO analysis of World Bank data.

Notes: According to the World Bank, data shown include only contracts reviewed by World Bank staff prior to award. In general, these types of contracts constitute about 40 percent of total World Bank investment lending. In addition, the nationality of a firm reflects the country in which it is registered, although the firm's parent may be headquartered in another country.

[a]Firms from at least 135 other countries won World Bank contracts, with firms from Ghana, Nigeria, Senegal, and Tanzania winning the largest numbers of contracts.

[b]Other contracts primarily represent contracts for goods such as transportation equipment, medical equipment and products, and information technology equipment.

U.S. Government Grants and Loans to Sub-Saharan Africa Have Increased since 2001, but China Does Not Publish Data on Its Financing

U.S. government development assistance, predominantly grants, to sub-Saharan Africa increased from $1.4 billion in 2001 to $9.2 billion in 2010 (see fig. 10).[57] This increase was driven primarily by growth in health assistance, resulting in part from the authorization of the President's Emergency Plan for AIDS Relief in 2003.[58] In 2010, health assistance and humanitarian aid were the largest categories of development assistance in sub-Saharan Africa.

---

[57]OECD defines official development assistance as those flows to countries and territories on the OECD's list of official development assistance recipients and to multilateral development institutions that are provided by official agencies, have the promotion of economic development and welfare of developing countries as their main objective, and are concessional and convey a grant element of at least 25 percent. According to U.S. aid data reported to OECD, U.S. development assistance to sub-Saharan Africa since 2008 has consisted of grants only. Between 2001 and 2010, less than 1 percent of annual U.S. development assistance to sub-Saharan Africa consisted of concessional loans for developmental purposes.

[58]Pub. L. No. 108-105. Through this program, the U.S. government has supported global HIV/AIDS prevention, treatment, and care.

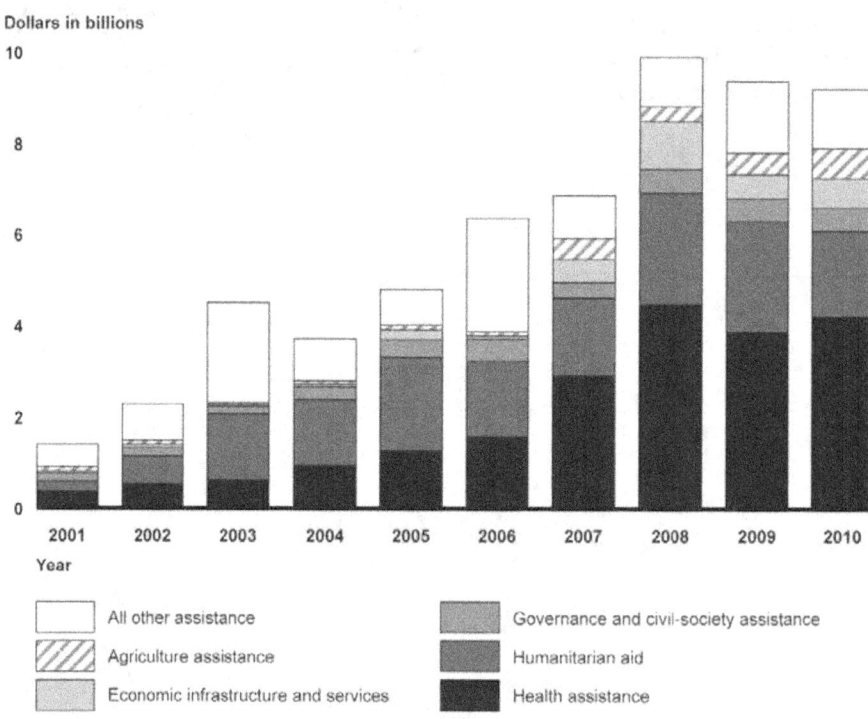

Figure 10: U.S. Government Development Assistance to Sub-Saharan Africa, 2001-2010

Source: GAO analysis of data from USAID.

Note: Amounts of aid represent commitments and are shown in nominal dollars. Data for 2011 were not available.

The Chinese government does not regularly report data on its development assistance to sub-Saharan Africa.[59] However, a white paper describing the Chinese government's foreign aid policy, published by the Information Office of China's State Council for the first time in 2011, states the value and type of development assistance provided worldwide.[60] According to the white paper, between 1950 and 2009, the

---

[59]The United States and other developed countries that are members of the OECD report aid data annually to the OECD, which makes this information publicly available. China is not an OECD member and does not report such data, although some nonmember countries, such as certain countries in the Persian Gulf, do report aid data to the OECD.

[60]Information Office of the State Council, People's Republic of China, "White Paper: China's Foreign Aid."

Chinese government provided $38.8 billion globally in grants, interest-free loans, and concessional loans as foreign aid, with the type of assistance varying by the scale of the project.[61] The white paper states that Chinese government grants are primarily for social welfare projects such as schools, hospitals, and water-supply projects; technical cooperation; and emergency humanitarian assistance, while the Chinese government's interest-free loans are primarily for construction of public facilities. The paper also states that the Chinese government's concessional loans are primarily for large and medium-sized infrastructure that generates economic and social benefits. An expert in China–Africa relations estimated that the Chinese government provided a total of about $6 billion in aid, including grants and concessional loans, to all of Africa between 2001 and 2009.[62]

U.S. government loans and related financing to support U.S-made products and firms' investments in sub-Saharan Africa increased from 2001 through 2011. U.S. Ex-Im's and OPIC's combined commitments, totaling more than $11.6 billion for this period, rose from an annual average of $858 million for 2001 through 2005 to $1.2 billion for 2006 through 2011.[63] The commitments varied considerably over this period. As figure 11 shows, U.S. Ex-Im's commitments ranged from $342 million in 2009 to about $1.7 billion in 2011, and OPIC's commitments ranged from about $149 million in 2002 to $948 million in 2011. During this period, U.S. Ex-Im financing was largely concentrated in Nigeria, South Africa, Ethiopia, Angola, Kenya, and Ghana, which represented 89 percent of Ex-Im financing committed for sub-Saharan Africa. For example, U.S. Ex-Im provided a direct loan of $806 million to a South African buyer for a U.S. firm's engineering services and provided loan guarantees of $605 million in Ethiopia and $256 million in Angola for

---

[61]To support Chinese-made products and firms' investments, the Chinese government also provides sub-Saharan African countries commercial loans that do not meet OECD's definition of development assistance.

[62]See Deborah Brautigam, *The Dragon's Gift*, app. 6. Dr. Brautigam calculated the Chinese government's estimated foreign aid using information from Chinese government sources, interviews, and extrapolations based on these sources.

[63]From 2001 to 2011, U.S. Ex-Im authorized about $ 7.2 billion in financing, including 72 percent for loan guarantees and loans, 23 percent for insurance, and 5 percent for working capital. During the same period, OPIC authorized approximately $3.3 billion in financing, including 70 percent for project financing, such as loans and loan guarantees, and 30 percent for insurance.

lenders' financing to Ethiopian and Angolan buyers of aircraft.[64] OPIC committed its largest amounts of financing in the region for projects such as oil and gas extraction, electric power generation, local banks, and medical equipment sales.

Figure 11: U.S. Government Loans and Related Financing Committed for U.S.-Made Products and U.S. Firms' Investments in Sub-Saharan Africa, 2001-2011

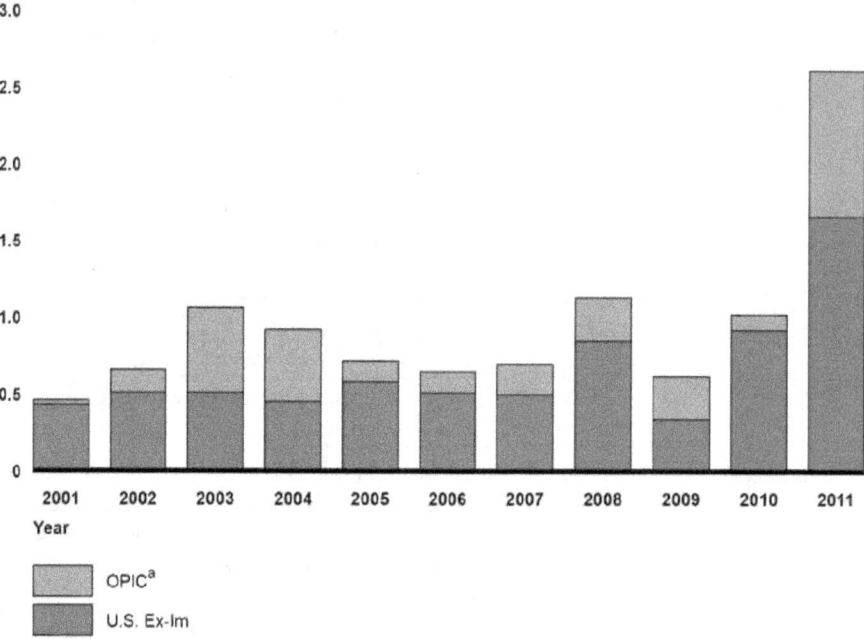

Source: GAO analysis of data from U.S. Ex-Im and OPIC.

Notes: Loans and other financing values are shown in nominal dollars by calendar year. In addition, these values are shown by calendar year, although U.S. Ex-Im and OPIC typically report data by fiscal year.

[a]OPIC may report data for some financing commitments, such as investment funds, only at the regional level. Data shown do not reflect OPIC investment funds for regional use in sub-Saharan Africa. OPIC's net commitments of regional investment funds to sub-Saharan Africa in fiscal years 2001 to 2011 amounted to $659.7 million. According to OPIC officials, because recipients of OPIC investment assistance may choose to invest in a set of countries, OPIC may initially lack information about the use of the assistance, such as the countries where such investments are made. In addition, according to OPIC officials, in countries with limited investment activity, business confidentiality agreements may prevent the disclosure of data that would reveal details of individual transactions.

---

[64]In providing such guarantees, U.S. Ex-Im promises to pay the lender if the buyer defaults.

The Chinese government does not publish data on its loans to sub-Saharan Africa.[65] However, according to a World Bank study as well as host-government officials in our case study countries, the Chinese government provides financing such as loans for infrastructure projects that promote the use of Chinese companies and materials.[66] In addition, Chinese officials have provided some general information on the government's loans to all of Africa. In a July 2012 interview with official Chinese media, the president of China Ex-Im stated that in the last 7 to 8 years, China Ex-Im completed about 600 projects and provided approximately $38 billion in loans for all of Africa. In contrast, U.S. Ex-Im authorized approximately $9.8 billion in loans and other financing for all of Africa in the last 8 years. In a May 2012 interview with official Chinese media, the vice president of China Development Bank's China-Africa Development Fund stated that by the end of 2008, the fund had invested about $400 million in 20 projects in Africa.

Reported U.S. Investment in Sub-Saharan Africa Exceeded China's Reported Investment for 2007 through 2011

Data on the United States' and China's investments in sub-Saharan Africa suggest that U.S. foreign direct investment flows exceeded China's reported foreign direct investment flows from 2007 through 2011.[67] During this period, U.S. foreign direct investment flows to sub-Saharan Africa were $16.6 billion and Chinese reported foreign direct investment flows were $12.7 billion.

---

[65]China is not a participant in the OECD Arrangement on Officially Supported Export Credits, an international agreement that governs various aspects of United States and other member countries' officially supported export credits. The agreement seeks to increase transparency among participants. Major industrialized countries are participants in this agreement. However, some countries with substantial export credit activity—including China and India—are not participants in the agreement. For more information, see GAO, *U.S. Export-Import Bank: Actions Needed to Promote Competitiveness and International Cooperation,* GAO-12-294 (Washington, D.C.: Feb. 7, 2012).

[66]See Vivien Foster et al. *Building Bridges: China's Growing Role as Infrastructure Financier for Africa* (Washington, D.C.: International Bank for Reconstruction and Development/World Bank, 2008).

[67]According to OECD, foreign direct investment is the ownership by a foreign person or business of 10 percent or more of the voting equity of a firm located in the host country. Foreign direct investment flows provide information for foreign direct investment activity within a given period of time, while foreign direct investment stock indicates the level of foreign direct investment at a given point in time.

Figure 12 shows reported annual foreign direct investment flows from the United States and China to sub-Saharan Africa in 2007 through 2011. According to experts, China's foreign direct investment flows are likely underreported and have other limitations.[68] The U.S. foreign direct investment flows shown in figure 12 are less than actual flows, in part because data for some countries in some years are confidential and have not been released; however, the data that have been released are considered generally reliable for the years and countries to which they pertain.

---

[68]China's reported foreign direct investment data represent official information published by the Chinese government and, despite their limitations, have been used in various reports, including those published by international organizations (such as IMF), government agencies, academic experts, and other research institutions, to describe China's foreign direct investment activities in Africa. The data appear to capture, for example, the Industrial and Commercial Bank of China's 2008 purchase of a 20 percent stake in South Africa's Standard Bank for about $4.8 billion.

Figure 12: Reported Flows of Foreign Direct Investment from the United States and China to Sub-Saharan Africa, 2007-2011

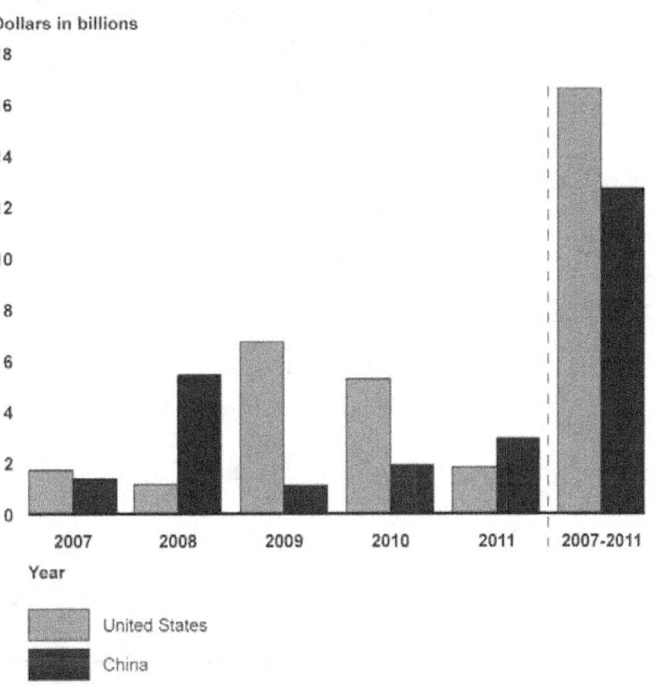

Dollars in billions

Year

Source: GAO analysis of data from BEA, China's Ministry of Commerce, China's National Bureau of Statistics, and Haver Analytics.

Notes: Although China has reported investment data since 2003, China did not include financial investment in its total investment data prior to 2007. According to experts, China's foreign direct investment flows are likely underreported and have other limitations. U.S. foreign direct investment flows shown are less than actual flows, in part because data for some countries in some years are confidential and have not been released. Foreign direct investment values are shown in nominal dollars.

As figure 12 shows, reported foreign direct investment flows to sub-Saharan Africa for the United States and China varied substantially during this period. For example, China's foreign direct investment flows increased significantly in 2008, in part because of the Industrial and Commercial Bank of China's purchase of 20 percent of South Africa's Standard Bank for about $4.8 billion. Also, U.S. foreign direct investment flows increased significantly in 2009, reflecting about $5 billion in flows to Nigeria.

For both the United States and China, the top sector for foreign direct investment was mining. According to the BEA, from 2006 through 2011, the largest share of U.S. foreign direct investment stock was in mining, with a significant portion tied to crude-oil extraction; other major sectors included finance and insurance, nonbank holding companies,[69] and manufacturing.[70] China does not publish data on foreign direct investment in sub-Saharan Africa by sector. However, according to the information office of China's State Council, the top three sectors of China's foreign direct investment stock in all of Africa by the end of 2009 were mining (29 percent), manufacturing (22 percent), and construction (16 percent).[71]

According to experts, China's data on foreign direct investment have several limitations that affect the reliability of these data.

- China's foreign direct investments in sub-Saharan Africa are likely underreported, according to experts. Chinese firms set up subsidiaries, in places such as Hong Kong and the British Virgin Islands, that can be used to make investments in sub-Saharan Africa. Such investments are not captured by China's data on foreign direct investment and may be a significant source of underreporting. In addition, many small and medium-sized enterprises may not register their foreign direct investments, which therefore may not be reflected in China's data.

The flow data reported for China's foreign direct investment are inconsistent with changes in the stock data, for reasons that are difficult to determine. For example, in 2008, China's foreign direct investment flow to sub-Saharan Africa was reported to be $5.4 billion; however, the change in foreign direct investment stock from the end of 2007 to the end of 2008 was reported to be -$1.6 billion, suggesting a difference of $7 billion between the flow and stock data. According to an IMF working paper, these variations between flows and stock are difficult to explain solely as a result of annual variation in the valuation of the foreign direct investment stock.[72]

---

[69]According to BEA, these nonbank holding companies generally had U.S. parent companies in mining, utilities, manufacturing (primarily petroleum related), and nonbank finance and insurance. A holding company typically does not produce goods or services itself but instead exists to own assets of other companies, which may be located in countries other than the holding company's.

[70]These sectors, with the exception of finance and insurance, also dominated U.S. foreign direct investment from 2001 through 2005.

[71]According to data from China's Ministry of Commerce, by the end of 2009, 88 percent of China's total foreign direct investment stock in Africa was in sub-Saharan Africa.

[72]See Montfort Mlachila and Misa Takebe, "FDI from BRICs to LICs: Emerging Growth Driver?" *IMF Working Paper*, WP/11/178 (2011), 11.

- China does not define foreign direct investment when reporting its data. However, the types of data China reports for its foreign direct investments (e.g., equity investment data, reinvested earnings data) are similar to data reported for U.S. foreign direct investment, which the United States defines on the basis of OECD's definition of foreign direct investment.

Although data on U.S. foreign investments are not complete, these data are generally considered reliable. Because of confidentiality, BEA has not released data on certain U.S. foreign direct investments in some countries for certain years. Additionally, according to BEA, U.S. firms, like Chinese firms, may use subsidiaries in other locations to make investments in sub-Saharan Africa that are not captured in the U.S. data on foreign direct investments to sub-Saharan Africa. In addition, the U.S. data may not include smaller firms. According to BEA, U.S. foreign investment data are based on a benchmark survey conducted in 2009, covering the value of all U.S. foreign direct investment. Moreover, U.S. foreign direct investment data do not show inconsistencies between flow data and changes in stock data to the same extent as China's data.

Angola, Ghana, and Kenya Illustrate Trends and Goals of U.S. and Chinese Engagement in Sub-Saharan Africa

The United States' and China's patterns of engagement in our three case-study countries reflect, to varying extents, broader trends in U.S. and Chinese engagement in sub-Saharan Africa as well as the two governments' goals and policies in the region. Similar to patterns for sub-Saharan Africa overall, crude oil imports have dominated both U.S. and Chinese trade in goods in Angola, and U.S. firms' total investments, driven by investments in the oil sector, have exceeded Chinese firms' total investments in Angola and Ghana. Also, Chinese government loans—mostly to facilitate Chinese firms' prominent role in infrastructure construction—have exceeded U.S. government financing in each of the case-study countries. Use of Chinese firms to implement projects funded through China's loans and grants is consistent with China's policy of mutual benefit in assisting African countries. U.S. officials expressed concern that some aspects of Chinese government loans, such as their lower cost and greater flexibility, may advantage Chinese firms over U.S. firms. However, direct competition between U.S. and Chinese firms in the case-study countries appears to be limited, although counterfeits manufactured by Chinese firms adversely affect U.S. firms' sales and reputation, especially in Kenya among our case study countries. Reflecting the U.S. goal of promoting development, and in contrast to the Chinese government providing financing primarily as loans, the U.S. government has provided increasing amounts of grants for health and humanitarian assistance in one country, Kenya, as it has in sub-Saharan Africa broadly. Finally, host-government requirements, such as regulations on hiring local labor, influence Chinese and U.S. firms' engagement in each case-study country.

Oil Imports Dominate U.S. and Chinese Trade with Angola, with U.S. Firms Investing Heavily in the Oil Sector in Angola and Ghana

As in other parts of sub-Saharan Africa, crude oil has accounted for most of U.S. and Chinese imports from Angola. Available data also show that U.S. firms' investments have been concentrated in the oil sector and exceeded Chinese firms' investments in Angola and Ghana, although the general nature of U.S. and Chinese investments in the sector differed. Kenya currently does not export oil, although some offshore and onshore oil exploration is under way.

U.S. and Chinese Imports

Imports of crude oil dominated overall U.S. and Chinese trade in goods with Angola from 2001 through 2011.[73] In 2011, crude oil imports accounted for 86 percent of U.S. trade in goods with Angola and 90 percent of China's goods trade. Figure 13 shows U.S. and Chinese imports of crude oil from Angola, as well as their total respective trade with Angola, in 2001 through 2011.

---

[73]In 2011, oil was also among the top categories of U.S. and Chinese imports from Ghana, although much smaller in magnitude than their imports from Angola. The absence of crude oil imports from Ghana prior to 2010 reflects the recent discovery and commercial production of crude oil in the country.

Figure 13: U.S. and Chinese Crude Oil Imports and Total Trade with Angola, 2001-2011

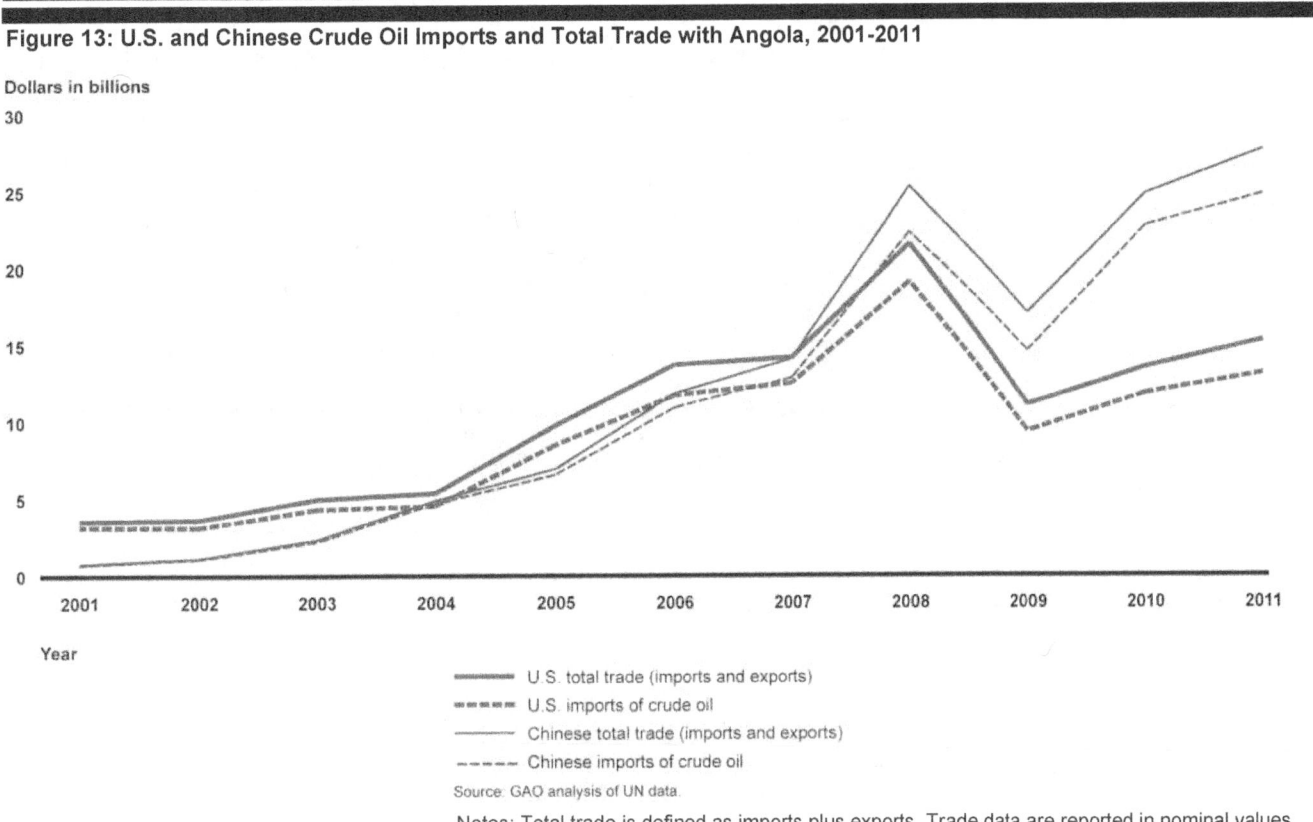

Dollars in billions

Year

——————— U.S. total trade (imports and exports)
▪ ▪ ▪ ▪ ▪ U.S. imports of crude oil
——————— Chinese total trade (imports and exports)
– – – – – Chinese imports of crude oil

Source: GAO analysis of UN data.

Notes: Total trade is defined as imports plus exports. Trade data are reported in nominal values. Changes in values over time are due in part to changes in the prices of traded goods.

Consistent with the overall trend for sub-Saharan Africa, oil was Angola's primary export to the United States under AGOA. Since 2004, crude oil has constituted almost 100 percent of Angola's exports to the United States under AGOA.[74]

U.S. and Chinese Investments

U.S. firms' investments in Angola have been predominantly in the oil sector, where they have greatly exceeded reported investments by Chinese firms. Although China does not publish data on its investments in

[74]From 2004, when Angola became eligible to export goods to the United States under AGOA, through 2011, more than half of U.S. oil imports from Angola received duty-free treatment under that program. During the same period, approximately 41 percent of U.S. oil imports from Angola received duty-free treatment under GSP. In 2011, nearly 87 percent of U.S. imports of oil from Angola received duty-free treatment under AGOA, while less than 3 percent of oil from Angola was imported under GSP.

countries by sectors, available data on U.S. and Chinese firms'
investments in Ghana show that U.S. firms' investments, primarily in oil
and other mining sectors, have also exceeded the total reported for
Chinese firms. Figure 14 shows U.S. and Chinese firms' cumulative
reported foreign direct investments in Angola and Ghana. For Angola,
data shown for both U.S. and Chinese firms' reported foreign direct
investments are from 2007 through 2011, the latest period for which
comparable data are available. For Ghana, Chinese firms' reported
foreign investments are shown for 2007 through 2011; U.S. data are
shown for 2010 to 2011, because BEA has not released confidential data
on U.S. foreign direct investments in the country from 2007 through 2009.

**Figure 14: U.S. and Chinese Firms' Cumulative Reported Foreign Direct
Investments in Angola and Ghana, 2007-2011**

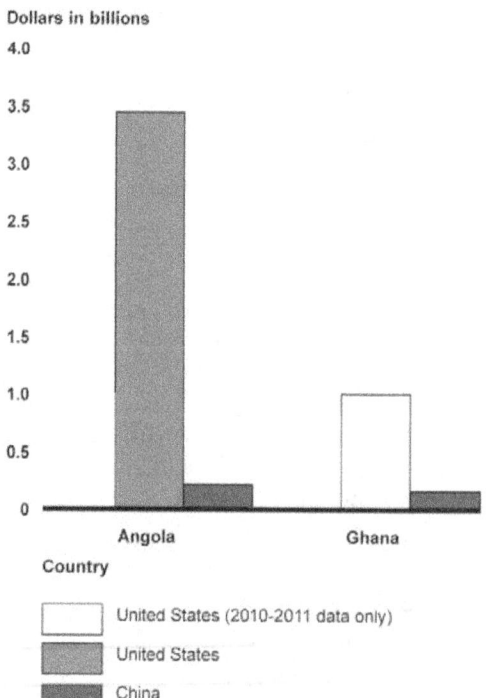

Source: GAO analysis of data from BEA and China's Ministry of Commerce.

Notes: BEA did not release U.S. foreign direct investment data for Ghana from 2007 to 2009 for
confidentiality reasons. According to experts, China's foreign direct investment data are likely
underreported.

Available data showing the extent of U.S. and Chinese firms' ownership
of oil blocks in Angola and Ghana provide some indication of their

respective investments in the oil sector.[75] According to these data, U.S. firms have invested both as operators and as nonoperators in the oil sector in Angola and Ghana, while Chinese firms have invested as nonoperators in Angola.[76] As of 2012, U.S. firms acted as operators for 11 of 49 oil blocks in Angola and for 2 of 17 oil blocks in Ghana.[77] As operators, they may have a minority stake but are primarily responsible for activities including drilling, maintenance, and ensuring compliance with required rules and regulations.[78] In addition, U.S. firms have purchased ownership interests in 5 oil blocks in Angola and 4 oil blocks in Ghana as nonoperators—that is, with a minority stake and no responsibility for operations. In contrast, Chinese firms have purchased ownership interests in 12 oil blocks in Angola as nonoperators. Firms from other countries —including Angola, Brazil, Denmark, France, Italy, Norway, and the United Kingdom, among others—also have operator and nonoperator roles in these oil blocks.[79] Figure 15 presents information on U.S. and Chinese firms' investments in oil blocks in Angola and Ghana.

[75]An oil block is a geographic area delineated by licensing authorities for oil exploration and production. The licensing authority grants exploration, production rights, or both, to an oil company or joint venture within the boundaries of the block, usually on an exclusive basis.

[76]According to a report by the U.S. Department of Energy's Energy Information Administration, Angola's national oil company, Sonangol, is the sole concessionaire and majority shareholder for oil and gas exploration and production in Angola and controls all petroleum industry activities. Sonangol works with foreign companies through joint ventures and production-sharing agreements. The Angolan government has plans under way to create a national oil agency that would act as regulator and concessionaire in place of Sonangol. Energy Information Administration, *Country Analysis Briefs: Angola* (Washington D.C.: 2011).

[77]Information on ownership of oil wells is as of September 2012 for Angola and as of August 2012 for Ghana.

[78]Angola has been a large oil producer for decades and is a member of the Organization of Petroleum Exporting Countries, while Ghana has been an oil producer since 2011. Additionally, in Angola, large international oil companies generally operate the country's oil wells; in Ghana, smaller independent oil firms operate the wells.

[79]No single foreign firm dominates Angola's oil sector, because the Angolan government generally distributes ownership stakes among multiple companies.

Figure 10: Number and Type of U.S and Chinese Firm Investments in Oil Blocks in Angola and Ghana as of 2011

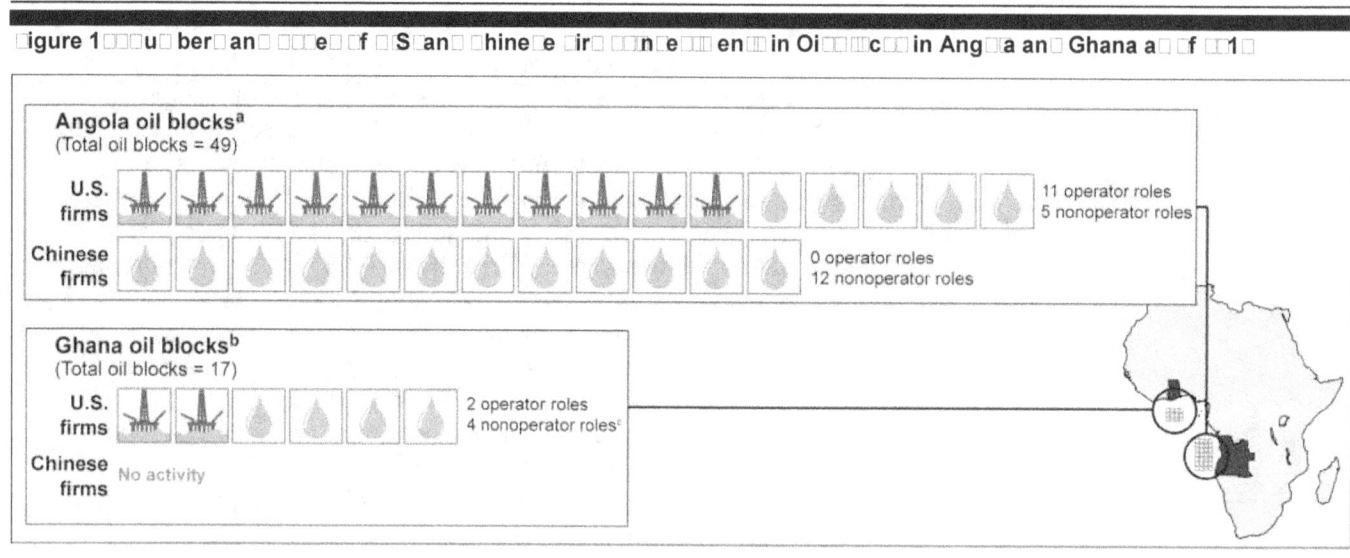

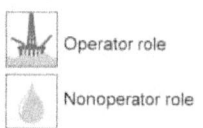
Operator role

Nonoperator role

Source: GAO analysis of information from the governments of Angola and Ghana (data); MapInfo (map).

Notes: An operator is generally the oil company that engages in drilling, service, and other operations; an operator has primary responsibility for maintaining well operations and ensuring compliance with required rules and regulations. A nonoperator generally has an ownership stake, similar to a minority and noncontrolling interest.

[a]In addition to U.S. firms, other firms, including firms from Angola, Brazil, France, Denmark, and the United Kingdom, operate Angola's 49 oil blocks.

[b]In addition to U.S. firms, other firms, including firms from Bermuda, Italy, Nigeria, and the United Kingdom, operate Ghana's 17 oil blocks. In one oil block, one U.S. firm had an operator role and another U.S. firm had a nonoperator role.

U.S. oil companies have an operator role in several oil blocks in Angola and Ghana because of the superior technological capability and management expertise required for complex offshore oil exploration and production operations, according to representatives from major oil firms and U.S. agency officials. In contrast, Chinese firms generally lack the technology and capacity to manage offshore oil operations.[80] However, as

---

[80]According to the Department of Energy, one Chinese national oil company recently launched its first deepwater drilling rig in the South China Sea. Additionally, Chinese national oil companies are gaining deepwater management experience as nonoperators and operators in other sub-Saharan African countries including Nigeria, Gabon, Equatorial Guinea, and Cameron, according to the Department of Energy.

nonoperators, Chinese firms can acquire project management experience by participating in decision making for oil well operations, according to a representative from another large oil firm.

Chinese firms have been willing to pay high prices to acquire ownership interest as nonoperators in Angola. According to a representative from a large U.S. oil company, in some instances Chinese firms have been willing to pay much higher prices than U.S. firms to purchase ownership interests, in part because Chinese firms are not answerable to shareholders and because they receive support, including financing, from the Chinese government. For example, the representative said, in 2008, no U.S. firm could match a Chinese firm's offer of $1 billion in "bonus" funds to purchase partial ownership in an oil block in Angola.[81] According to a representative from another large U.S. oil firm, Chinese firms do not consider the cost and profitability of their oil sector purchases in the same manner as Western firms, because Chinese state-owned firms may view these purchases as a means of meeting the Chinese government's strategic objective of securing oil supply.[82]

The Chinese Government Has Provided More Loans Than the U.S. Government, Primarily for Construction by Chinese Firms

Available data indicate that Chinese government loans to the governments of all three case-study countries—primarily for infrastructure construction by Chinese firms—have exceeded U.S. government loans. The Chinese government has also provided a small amount of grants, mostly for construction projects. The tying of loans and grants to the use of Chinese firms is consistent with China's policy of seeking mutual benefit in assisting African countries with infrastructure development; however, U.S. officials are concerned that China's loans may disadvantage U.S. firms. In addition to financing from the Chinese government, funding from other donors, including the United States, has supported Chinese firms' infrastructure construction projects.

---

[81]Oil companies typically offer "bonuses" in addition to royalty fees to acquire ownership rights in oil blocks.

[82]China's national interest in securing oil supplies has led the Chinese national oil companies to invest throughout the world, according to the Department of Energy.

Chinese Government Loans Exceed U.S. Government Loans and Benefit Chinese Firms

Available data indicate that Chinese government loans and related financing to Angola, Ghana, and Kenya have exceeded U.S. government loans and related financing.[83] As figure 16 shows, Chinese government credit lines to Angola from 2002 through 2011 exceeded U.S. loans and related financing by more than $11 billion, Chinese government loans to Ghana from 2006 through 2011 exceeded U.S. loans and related financing by more than $2.4 billion, and Chinese government loans to Kenya from July 2009 through June 2012 exceeded U.S. government loans and related financing by more than $77 million.[84] Chinese government loans and related financing were primarily for infrastructure projects, such as construction of roads, rail, hospitals, schools, housing, and water and energy infrastructure, to be implemented by Chinese firms, including state-owned firms.[85] U.S. officials observed that China's infrastructure construction addresses a key need in Africa. In contrast to Chinese loans and related financing, U.S. government loans and related financing generally have supported private-sector and host-government purchases of U.S. exports, including aircraft and machinery, through U.S. Ex-Im, as well as investments in loan portfolios, geothermal energy, and medical equipment through OPIC. U.S. agencies such as U.S. Ex-Im and OPIC offer loans and related financing for specific transactions intended to increase U.S. exports or benefit U.S. firms' investments.

[83]In addition to loans, China has committed credit lines in some cases. A borrower draws funds from a credit line, incurring a loan. U.S. government agencies such as U.S. Ex-Im and OPIC provide loans as well as loan guarantees and insurance.

[84]We obtained data on China's loans to Angola from information published by the Angolan Ministry of Finance and from a U.S. official. Other sources corroborated data on China's total lending and provided some additional information about its loans to Angola. Additionally, we obtained information about China's loans and grants to Ghana and Kenya from documents published by the Ghanaian and Kenyan governments. Data on China's loans were available for different time periods in each of the case-study countries. China does not publish country-specific data on its loans and grants.

[85]A joint study by the World Bank and the Chinese government states that China's state-owned enterprises and government are closely connected and that Chinese state-owned enterprises are more likely to receive preferential access to bank finance, privileged access to business opportunities, and even protection against competition. See World Bank and Development Research Center of the State Council, People's Republic of China, *China 2030: Building a Modern, Harmonious, and Creative High-Income Society.*

Figure 1: Available Data on U.S. Government and Chinese Government Loan and Related Financing Commitments for Angola, Ghana, and Kenya

Years[a]	Loans and related financing commitments,[b] dollars in billions		Examples of projects financed	
			U.S. government	Chinese government
2002-2011	Angola	$0.68 12.00	Aerospace products and parts, expansion of small and medium-sized enterprise loan portfolio, building materials manufacturing	Roads, rail, airports, housing, water supply, hospitals, schools, telecommunications, boats
2006-2011	Ghana[c]	0.95 3.35	Engineered wood products, architectural and engineering services, medical equipment, residential home mortgage loans	Oil and gas infrastructure, rail, roads, ports, irrigation, dam construction, e-government
2009-2012[d]	Kenya	0.41 0.48	Aerospace products and parts, geothermal power project, microfinance portfolio	Roads, geothermal wells, power distribution, telecommunications

▢ U.S. government

▢ Chinese government

Source: GAO analysis of data from OPIC, U.S. Ex-Im, U.S. officials, experts, and governments of Ghana and Kenya.

[a]Data on Chinese government loans and related financing for each country were available only for the indicated periods. Although data on U.S. government loans and related financing are available for prior years, U.S. government commitments are shown only for the indicated periods.

[b]U.S. government commitments include loans and related financing such as loan guarantees and insurance. Chinese government commitments include credit lines as well as loans. In Angola, China committed credit lines, from which a borrower can draw funds, incurring a loan.

[c]The Ghanaian government published data on China's loan commitments as of September of each year in its annual budget documents for 2006 through 2011. Available budget data did not include China's $3 billion loan to Ghana signed in December 2011. We have included the $3 billion loan with previous loan commitments because this financing represents China's most significant loan package to Ghana.

[d]U.S. government and Chinese government loans and related financing commitments are presented for Kenya's fiscal years, from July 2009 through June 2012, because data for China were only available for this period.

The government of China has generally committed loans and credit lines to support Chinese firms' infrastructure construction in the three case-study countries through high-level agreements with each country's government. For example:

- *Angola*. The Chinese government's commitments of about $12 billion in credit lines to the Angolan government in 2002 through 2011 have driven much of Chinese firms' engagement in the country, according to U.S. and Angolan officials.[86]

- *Ghana*. The Chinese government signed a $3 billion loan agreement with the Ghanaian government in December 2011 for 12 eligible infrastructure projects to be implemented primarily by Chinese firms,[87] according to Ghana's finance ministry.[88]

- *Kenya*. The Chinese government's commitments of about $480 million in loans, mostly for infrastructure construction, between July 2009 and June 2012 were generally provided under agreements between the Chinese and Kenyan governments. According to Kenyan finance ministry officials, these agreements identified Chinese firms that would implement loan-financed projects.

Chinese government loans and related financing for projects in Africa have enabled Chinese firms to establish and expand operations within the region. For example, according to officials from an Angolan nongovernmental organization (NGO), Chinese state-owned enterprises and, later, Chinese private-sector firms began operating in Angola after the Chinese government agreed to provide loans to the Angolan government following the conclusion of the country's civil war in 2002. According to Kenyan officials, China's investments in Kenya have increased, in part because some Chinese firms that initially came to Kenya to work on Chinese government–financed projects have diversified into other sectors.

---

[86]Comprehensive information on disbursement of China's credit lines and loans to Angola is not available. However, data published by the Angolan Ministry of Finance indicates that as of June 2008 about 30 percent China's credit lines of $2 billion in 2004 and $2.5 billion in 2007 were disbursed.

[87]U.S. officials said that they questioned how much of China's $3 billion loan commitment to Ghana in December 2011 will be disbursed. Although disbursement information for this loan is not yet available, data published by Ghana's Ministry of Finance and Economic Planning for the construction of the Bui hydroelectric dam indicate that as of September 2011, almost $129 million (70 percent) of the nearly $185 million committed by the Chinese government had been disbursed since 2008.

[88]In 2006 and 2011, the Chinese government also committed about $353 million to the Ghanaian government for several projects, including dam construction, communication infrastructure and systems, and electrification.

In addition providing loans, the Chinese government has also provided small amounts of grant assistance, primarily for infrastructure such as hospitals, government buildings, and sports stadiums that were built by Chinese firms. For example, China committed almost $39 million in grant funding to Kenya from July 2009 through June 2012 for construction projects including roads, a sports stadium, and a hospital, according to Kenyan government reports on donor funding. In 2011, China committed $15 million in grants for the construction of Ghana's Ministry of Foreign Affairs' building, according to Ghanaian government budget reports.[89]

U.S. Officials Are Concerned That Chinese Government Loans May Disadvantage U.S. Firms

U.S. officials from several agencies expressed concerns that some aspects of Chinese government loans—their lower cost, greater flexibility, and lack of transparency—may advantage Chinese firms over U.S. firms.

- *Lower cost.* Our analysis of information on specific Chinese government infrastructure loans to Angola, Ghana, and Kenya showed that borrowers' costs for these loans have generally been less than borrowers' costs for U.S. government loans to Angola and Kenya, and, to a lesser extent, to Ghana (see app. II for more details).[90] The Chinese government loans that we analyzed generally required a lower repayment over time, in terms of net present value, than would a U.S. government loan for a similar project.[91] For example, compared with China Ex-Im's and China Development Bank's November 2009 loans of $6 billion and $1.5 billion, respectively, to Angola, the repayment required for a hypothetical U.S. Ex-Im loan to Angola at the same time and of the same size would be greater because of factors such as higher fees (7.62 percent up-front fees for the U.S. Ex-Im loan vs. 0.25 percent fees for the China Ex-Im and China Development Bank loans) and a shorter repayment period

---

[89]No published information is available regarding China's grants to Angola.

[90]In addition, our analysis of information on specific Chinese government infrastructure loans to Angola, Ghana, and Kenya showed that these loans are more costly than World Bank loans to Ghana and Kenya, but not to Angola.

[91]Because U.S. Ex-Im did not offer loans for the construction sector during a similar period as the Chinese loans, U.S. Ex-Im provided us terms for hypothetical loans for the construction sector for the same country, on the same date, and of the same magnitude as the Chinese government loans.

(5 years for the U.S. Ex-Im loan vs. 15 years for the China Ex-Im loan and 8 years for the China Development Bank loan).[92]

- *Greater flexibility.* China's loans may provide more flexible terms for the use of local content such as labor and materials, making them more attractive to host-country governments. U.S. Ex-Im finances the purchase of goods originated and shipped from the United States and also finances U.S.-provided services. In addition to financing U.S. exports, U.S. Ex-Im may in some cases provide financing for local costs, such as local labor and materials, up to 30 percent of the contract value of the export.[93] U.S. Ex-Im authorized more than $70 million for local costs in Ghana between 2001 and 2011, equal to about 10 percent of its export financing for Ghana. Under its recent $3 billion loan agreement with Ghana, China agreed to finance 60 percent Chinese content and up to 40 percent Ghanaian content, according to a senior Ghanaian government official.[94]

- *Lack of transparency.* U.S. officials and others noted that, in general, the Chinese government's engagement with African countries lacks transparency. According to U.S. officials, in some cases the lack of transparency regarding aspects of Chinese government loans, such as their amount, terms, and purpose, may limit the U.S. government's ability to provide competitive loans to support the purchase of U.S. exports, thus affecting U.S. firms' ability to compete with Chinese

[92]We obtained information about loans such as the amount, interest rate, maturity, and repayment period. When we could not obtain information about specific loan terms, such as the disbursement periods and the commitment fees for China's loans to Angola and Kenya, we made assumptions on the basis of comparable loans' terms or as appropriate. The repayment value of loans can differ on the basis of each loan's interest rate, maturity, and other fees. According to U.S. Ex-Im officials, U.S. Ex-Im's fees reflect risk of the borrower's defaulting on the loan and are based on country risk, the risk classification of the borrower, the terms of the loan, and the disbursement period.

[93]Under OECD rules, U.S. Ex-Im can provide up to 30 percent financing for local costs for medium- and long-term transactions if these expenses are related to the U.S. exporter's scope of work and if the U.S. exporter has demonstrated that local cost support is available from a competitor export credit agency or that private market financing of local costs was difficult to obtain for the transaction. Between 2001 and 2011, U.S. Ex-Im committed more than $70 million for financing local costs in Ghana and committed an additional $1.2 million in Nigeria. Information on large Chinese government loans indicates that China requires between 60 and 70 percent Chinese content.

[94]Chinese content includes materials made in China as well as Chinese labor to implement projects in the host country.

firms' costs of products and services. For instance, according to U.S. Ex-Im officials, absence of information on the cost of China's loans may prevent U.S. Ex-Im from offering competitive loans for U.S. exports and may thus disadvantage U.S. firms interested in exporting their goods and services. According to agency officials, U.S. Ex-Im adheres to OECD rules, which in rare cases allow a participant export credit agency to match a non-OECD participant's financing terms and conditions, if there is evidence or specific information about the non-OECD country's financing offer. However, according to U.S. Ex-Im, such information is typically difficult to obtain from the borrower, who is the potential beneficiary of the better terms. Moreover, because the Chinese government is generally not transparent in its lending practices, according to U.S. Ex-Im officials, it is difficult to obtain specific information on China's financing terms and U.S. Ex-Im can rarely use this OECD provision.[95]

Other Donors Have Also Financed Construction by Chinese Firms

Funding provided by other donors, such as the World Bank and the United States through MCC, has supported construction projects for which Chinese firms have competed in the case-study countries.[96] For example, according to data on World Bank-funded contracts in the three case-study countries, Chinese firms won about $455 million in contracts for construction projects.[97] In Ghana, the only one of our three case-study countries to qualify for an MCC compact, Chinese firms won about $112 million in contracts (22 percent of overall MCC-Ghana contract dollars) for construction projects. Chinese firms are also heavily engaged in construction contracts for the African Development Bank in Kenya,

---

[95]In one instance, according to U.S. Ex-Im, it was able to obtain information to match China's loan offer for a rail project in Pakistan in 2010.

[96]MCC signed a 5-year, $547 million agreement or compact with Ghana that began in 2007. The MCC compact provided grants to fund agriculture, transportation, and rural services projects, including the construction of postharvest infrastructure such as a cargo center and packhouses, upgrades to a major highway and other roads, and improvements to the rural electrification infrastructure.

[97]Construction projects accounted for 89 percent of overall contract dollars won by Chinese firms for World Bank-funded projects.

according to one donor official.[98] Figure 17 shows examples of Chinese firms' construction projects in Angola, Ghana, and Kenya.

---

[98]According to a report published by the World Bank in 2008, Chinese firms won more than 30 percent, by value, of construction contracts financed by the World Bank and African Development Bank in Africa from 2004 through 2006, making Chinese firms more successful than contractors of any other nationality. Furthermore, since 1999, China's construction sector has seen annual growth of 20 percent, making China the largest construction market in the global economy. See Vivian Foster et al., *Building Bridges: China's Growing Role as Infrastructure Financier for Africa* (Washington, D.C.: International Bank for Reconstruction and Development/World Bank, 2008).

Figure 1: Examples of Construction Projects Implemented by Chinese Firms in Angola, Ghana, and Kenya

Source: GAO.

Housing units near Luanda, Angola, being constructed by Chinese firms, according to a U.S. official.

Source: GAO.

Nairobi–Thika Highway, built by three Chinese state-owned firms and funded by the African Development Bank and the Chinese government in Kenya.

Source: GAO.

Accra Sports Stadium, the primary soccer arena in Accra, Ghana, renovated by a Chinese firm for the 2008 Africa Cup of Nations.

Chinese firms are competitive in the construction sector in part because their business practices keep construction costs low, according to officials from U.S. and host-country governments and other donor organizations. For example, Chinese firms house workers near project sites and maintain long work days. According to some host-government officials, because Chinese firms are engaged in infrastructure development in other parts of Africa, their cost of moving materials and equipment to new project sites may be lower than that of other firms. An official from a donor organization in Kenya noted that Chinese firms have bid below estimates developed by independent engineers who assessed costs for donor-funded projects.

Competition between U.S. and Chinese Firms and Products Has Been Limited

U.S. and Chinese firms and products largely operate in different, noncompeting sectors in the three case-study countries, aside from their operations in the information and technology sector. U.S. and Chinese firms also face limited competition in part because U.S. firms are less willing to conduct business in some areas of sub-Saharan Africa, citing factors such as business risk and market size. In addition, counterfeits manufactured by Chinese firms adversely affect U.S. firms' sales and reputation in Kenya.

U.S. and Chinese Firms Generally Operate in Different Sectors

U.S. and Chinese firms and products generally operate in different sectors, with the exception of the information and communications sector, according to officials from U.S. agencies and U.S. firms in the three case-study countries. For example, U.S. officials in Angola noted that U.S. firms are active primarily in the oil and gas sector, while Chinese firms are active in the construction sector.[99] Similarly, U.S. officials and host-government officials in Ghana stated that U.S. firms are generally more engaged in higher-technology sectors, while Chinese firms are most active in infrastructure construction. Moreover, according to Commerce officials, anecdotal evidence suggests that U.S. firms are choosing not to compete for projects such as major infrastructure construction for which they perceive competition with Chinese firms to be extremely difficult.

Data on World Bank– and MCC-funded contracts illustrate U.S. and Chinese firms' operations in noncompeting sectors. In all three case-

---

[99]Although Chinese firms have invested in Angola's oil sector, they have done so in a nonoperator role. In contrast, U.S. firms have an operator role in several oil blocks in Angola.

study countries, U.S. firms won a small share of the combined value of these donor-funded contracts, primarily for consulting services, while Chinese firms won a much larger share of these contracts' combined value, primarily for construction services. In Ghana, the only case-study country to qualify for an MCC compact, no U.S. firms bid on MCC contracts for construction projects, according to officials who oversaw MCC contracts in Ghana, while Chinese firms won about $112 million in contracts (22 percent of overall MCC contract dollars), all for construction projects.[100] Similarly, in all three countries, Chinese firms won a large share of World Bank–financed construction contracts but won a very small share of consulting contracts.[101] Figure 18 shows World Bank–financed contracts won by U.S. and Chinese firms, as well as firms from other countries, in Angola, Ghana, and Kenya from 2001 to 2011.

[100]Portuguese firms won the highest amount of MCC construction contracts in Ghana, by nationality, with a total of almost $114 million in contracts. Ghanaian firms were the top contractor by nationality overall, with a total of $192 million in contracts.

[101]Services provided by U.S. firms under World Bank-funded contracts represent a small fraction (less than 1 percent) of annual U.S. trade in service exports to Angola, Ghana, and Kenya. However, World Bank contracts represent one of the few instances where data are available for examination of potential competition between U.S. and Chinese firms. According to the World Bank, the data include only contracts reviewed by World Bank staff prior to award, which comprise about 40 percent of total World Bank investment lending. The nationality of a firm reflects the country where it is registered, although the firm's parent may be headquartered in another country.

Figure 19: World Bank-Financed Contracts with U.S., Chinese, and Other Firms in Angola, Ghana, and Kenya, 2001-2011

Firm's country of origin	Number of contracts	World Bank contract dollars won, percentage	Contract value by categories, dollars in millions			Top three contract types, number of contracts
United States	60	1	$14 $0 $9			Management/technical advice .... 16 Equipment, information technology ..... 9 Feasibility studies 5
China	66	21	$1	$455	$56	Equipment, electrical .... 15 Construction services, maintenance ..... 13 and rehabilitation Equipment, medical 10
Other countries[a]	1,943	78	$346	$1,038	$462	Management/technical advice .... 260 Construction services, infrastructure ..... 182 Equipment, transportation 150

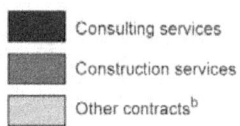

■ Consulting services

■ Construction services

□ Other contracts[b]

Source: GAO analysis of World Bank data.

Notes: According to the World Bank, the data shown include only contracts reviewed by World Bank staff prior to award. In general, these types of contracts constitute about 40 percent of total World Bank investment lending. The nationality of a firm reflects the country where it is registered, although the firm's parent may be headquartered in another country.

[a]Firms from at least 52 other countries won World Bank contracts, with firms from Angola, Ghana, and Kenya winning the most contracts.

[b]Other contracts primarily include contracts to provide goods such as transportation equipment, medical equipment and products, and information technology equipment.

Data from Commerce provide some evidence that European firms have been U.S. firms' primary competitors for host-country government contracts in our case-study countries. From August 2002 to February 2012, U.S. firms requested assistance from Commerce's Advocacy Center in competing for 47 host-government contracts for goods and services in Angola, Ghana, and Kenya. Chinese firms competed for 9 of these contracts, mostly in Ghana and Kenya, for telecommunications, computers and information technology, and transportation services (see fig. 19). French, German, and British firms competed with U.S. firms for more of the contracts and in more sectors, including oil and gas, energy and power, aerospace, and telecommunications, than did Chinese firms.

Figure 19☐☐a☐na☐i☐☐☐f ☐ir☐ ☐☐☐☐ ☐e☐ing f☐r 4☐ Ang☐an ☐ Ghanaian ☐an☐ ☐en☐an G☐☐ern☐☐en☐☐☐n☐rac☐☐☐☐☐-☐1☐

Sectors in which firms completed

		Number of contracts for which at least one firm completed	Computers, information technology, and security	Aerospace	Energy and power	Oil and gas	Telecommunications	Transportation	Services	Other	Healthcare	Infrastructure	Heavy machinery
United States (total)		47	7	6	6	5	5	4	4	4	3	2	1
Other firms competing for the same contracts as U.S. firms	China	9	2			1	2	2		1	1		
	France	15	1		4		4	3		2	1		
	Germany	11	1	1			3	1		3		1	1
	United Kingdom	10	3	1		3	2			1			

Source: GAO analysis of Department of Commerce data.

Notes: Data shown are for 47 contracts for which U.S. firms requested Department of Commerce advocacy assistance in August 2002 through February 2012. Firms from France, Germany, and the United Kingdom competed with U.S. firms for the largest numbers of contracts.

U.S. and Chinese firms' competition in information technology and telecommunications was particularly noted by U.S. officials and U.S. firms in Kenya, although it is unclear whether this competition directly affects U.S.-made exports to these countries. For instance, a senior official at a large U.S. information and communications technology firm noted that Chinese firms are innovating and adapting quickly to local markets, such as in Kenya, where a Chinese firm in this sector has established one of Kenya's largest training centers.[102] In addition, trade data indicate that China's exports of telecommunications equipment to Kenya rose from

---

[102]In addition, according to the U.S. firm official, both the Chinese government and European governments are more active than the U.S. government in combining government and business interests to take advantage of large telecommunications projects in countries such as Kenya.

$0.5 million in 2001 to $122 million in 2011. However, the extent to which direct competition from Chinese firms affects U.S.-made exports is unclear, in part because multinational corporations headquartered in the United States operate and export globally. For example, according to a representative of a U.S. firm that manufactures telecommunications equipment, because most of its products are manufactured outside the United States, competition from Chinese telecommunications firms does not affect its U.S.-made exports.

Business Risk and Market Size Limit U.S.-Chinese Competition

Competition between U.S. and Chinese firms may be limited in part by U.S. firms' hesitation to conduct business in parts of sub-Saharan Africa, owing to factors such as business risk and market size. According to U.S. and host-country officials, U.S. firms are less willing than Chinese firms to risk investments in sectors other than oil and gas because U.S. firms are concerned about risks associated with conducting business in the region, such as corruption and a lack of economic and political stability. For example, according to a senior representative from a U.S. firm in Kenya, the business environment in Kenya, and in East Africa broadly, lacks the regulatory and structural framework to which U.S. firms are accustomed. U.S. firms prefer limited risk and moderate growth, whereas Africa overall is a higher-risk and higher-growth market, according to the U.S. firm representative. In addition, U.S. and Ghanaian officials stated that markets such as Ghana are often too small to be cost-effective for U.S. firms' operations and that these firms are therefore unwilling to invest. In contrast to U.S. firms, Chinese firms are more willing to be flexible in commercial dealings—for example, collaborating with local businesses—and to take on business risk, according to business representatives and U.S. officials in Kenya and Ghana. Some officials stated that this willingness results in part from Chinese government financing, which helps offset risks that other firms must face independently and which eases decision making in the absence of accountability to shareholders.

Chinese Counterfeits Have Negatively Affected U.S. Firms

Counterfeit goods and related products from China have adversely affected U.S. firms' sales and reputation, especially in Kenya among our case-study countries.[103] According to a 2012 study by the Kenyan

---

[103]According to a March 2012 draft report by the Kenyan Association of Manufacturers, counterfeiting includes the violation of trademarks, industrial designs, geographical indications, copyright, and related rights. Kenyan Association of Manufacturers, *The Study to Determine Severity of the Counterfeit Problem In Kenya as It Affects Industries and Impact of Proliferation of Counterfeit Products from Other EAC Partner States And Far East Countries Into the Kenyan Market,* draft report (March 2012).

Association of Manufacturers, counterfeit goods primarily from China, especially in the energy, electronic, and electrical components sectors, have negatively affected the sales and reputation of U.S. firms and others with operations in Kenya.[104] For example, a representative of a U.S. firm that manufactures batteries in Kenya noted that an influx of counterfeit and substandard products, mainly from China, caused the U.S. firm's business to decline and that over time the firm has decreased the number of its employees in Kenya from 800 to 300.[105] In some cases, Chinese products, although of poorer quality, also mimicked the U.S. firm's product branding and color schemes, according to a former senior executive of this U.S. firm. The former executive noted that although the U.S. firm successfully litigated in Kenyan courts against this trademark infraction, the penalty was too lenient to have a deterrent effect on the Chinese manufacturers. In another instance, a representative of a large U.S. firm with regional headquarters in Kenya stated that the Chinese theft of intellectual property, in general, is one of the biggest challenges that U.S. firms face in Africa.[106] To combat Chinese counterfeits, the U.S. embassy in Kenya has sponsored several public-education programs, and the U.S. government is providing technical assistance to Kenya's Anti-Counterfeit Agency, established in 2010.

---

[104]The Kenyan Association of Manufacturers report on counterfeits notes that counterfeit products result in a loss of revenue for manufacturers in Kenya as well as for the Kenyan government. The report cited a senior Kenyan official's statement that Kenyan manufacturers incur a net loss of more than $40 million and that the Kenyan government loses about $80 million in tax revenue annually as a result of counterfeit products. According to manufacturers interviewed for that report, about 30 percent of electrical components and electronics (e.g., motors, generators, switchgears, and batteries) are counterfeits and are primarily from China. See Kenyan Association of Manufacturers, *The Study to Determine Severity of the Counterfeit Problem.*

[105]Trade data indicate that China's exports of batteries (including rechargeable batteries and parts) increased from $15 million in 2001 to $48 million in 2011.

[106]Although China and African countries have initiated efforts to combat counterfeits and protect intellectual property rights, the success of these efforts is unclear, according to Commerce officials.

U.S. Government Engagement in Kenya Illustrates Strong Focus on Aid

Similar to overall U.S. aid trends for sub-Saharan Africa, and in keeping with the U.S. goal to support development in the region, the U.S. government has provided generally increasing amounts of development assistance, predominantly grants, to Kenya, primarily driven by health and humanitarian assistance (see fig. 20).[107] From 2001 to 2010, the United States committed almost $4 billion in development assistance to Kenya.[108]

---

[107]According to U.S. aid data reported to OECD, concessional loans constituted less than 0.1 percent of U.S. aid to Kenya from 2001 through 2010. The United States has not committed any loans as aid to Kenya since 2008.

[108]During the same period, the United States committed about $1.6 billion in development assistance to Ghana as part of an MCC compact starting in 2007. This assistance differed from U.S. assistance to Kenya in its focus on infrastructure and agriculture projects. For more information on MCC-funded projects in Ghana see the supplemental report GAO-13-280SP. Compared to Kenya and Ghana, the United States committed a smaller amount of aid to Angola—about $804 million—during the same period because the United States discontinued humanitarian assistance to Angola.

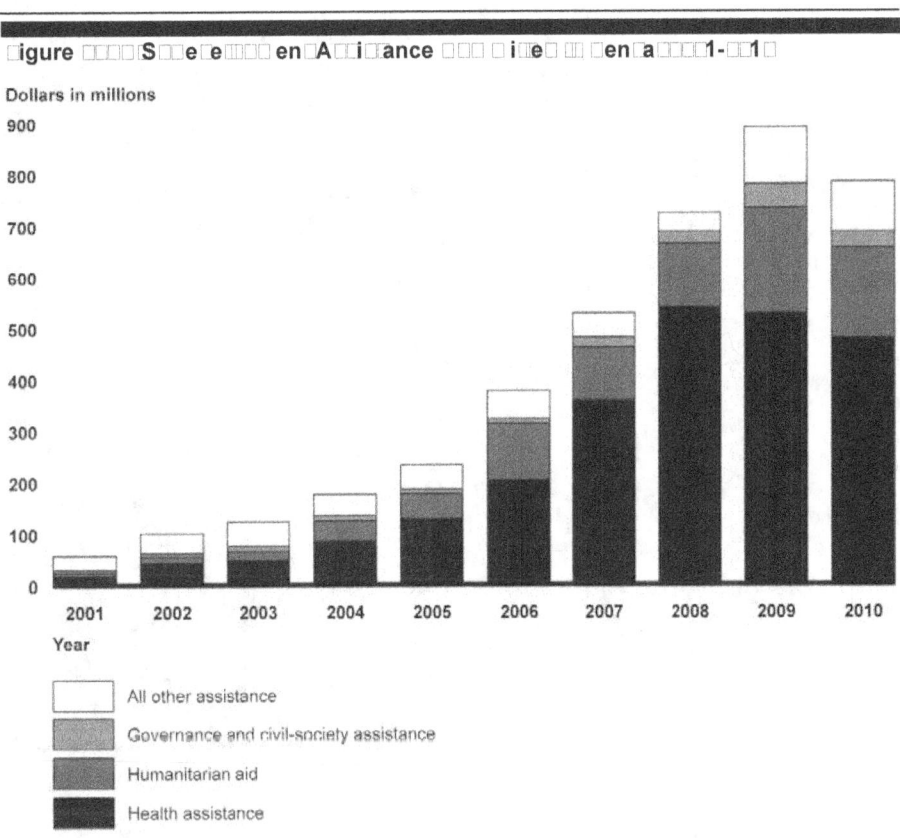

Figure ___: S__e__e___en_A__i_ance ___ _i_e_ __ _en_a___1-__1_

Dollars in millions

All other assistance
Governance and civil-society assistance
Humanitarian aid
Health assistance

Source: GAO analysis of data from USAID.

Note: Data are reported in nominal dollars.

U.S. aid to Kenya also included assistance for building trade capacity. From 2001 to 2011, about 96 percent of U.S. imports from Kenya under AGOA consisted of apparel, textiles, leather, and footwear (see fig. 21). AGOA's "third-country fabric" provision has enabled Kenya to increase its apparel exports generally, according to U.S. and Kenyan officials, and Kenya has become one of the largest sub-Saharan African exporters of nonpetroleum goods to the United States under AGOA. U.S. and Kenyan officials pointed to the positive employment effects in Kenya associated with apparel exports under AGOA. However, they also noted AGOA's limited success in enabling Kenya and other sub-Saharan African countries to manufacture the textiles and fabrics that form the input for apparel manufacturing. Kenya and Ghana obtain fabrics mostly from

China and other Asian countries to manufacture apparel for export to the United States, according to U.S. officials in these countries.[109] Chinese exports of textile and fabrics to Kenya grew during this period from $40 million in 2001 to $347 million in 2011.

Figure 1 S   r fr   en a un er AGOA   1- 11

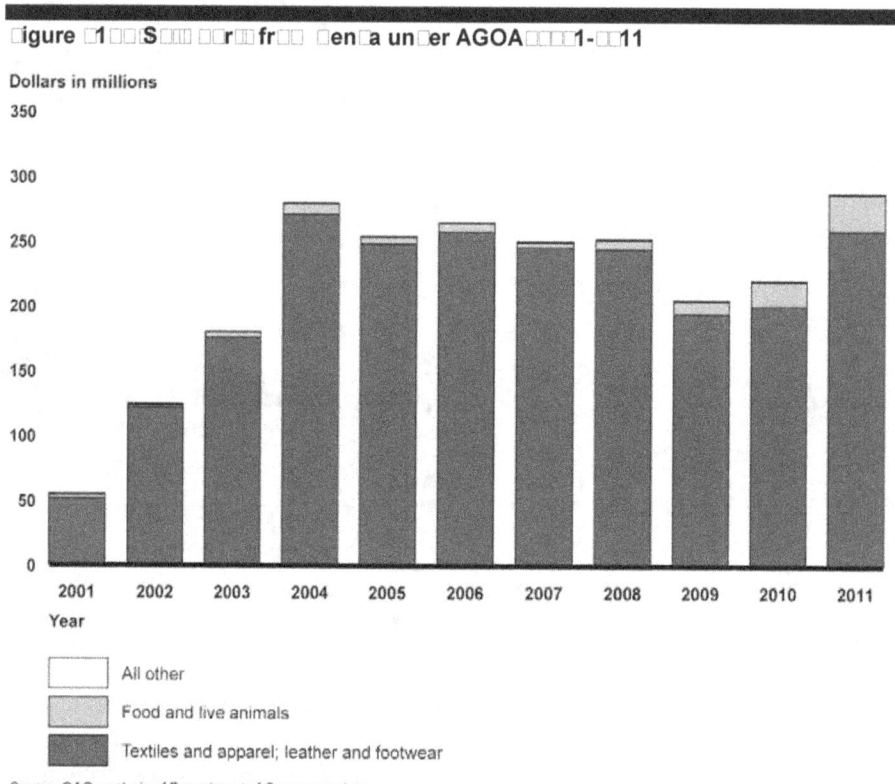

Source: GAO analysis of Department of Commerce data.

Note: Data are reported in nominal dollars.

---

[109]According to U.S. officials in Kenya, about 90 percent of Kenya's apparel exports are made of imported fabric. Specifically, about half of the imported fabric is from China (mostly woven fabrics) and Taiwan (mostly higher-end fabrics), and the remainder is from India and Pakistan (mostly knits from both countries).

Limited available data suggest that, in contrast to U.S. aid, China's aid as grants to Kenya was relatively small.[110] Moreover, U.S. officials stated that projects supported by China's grants—primarily infrastructure projects—are different from those supported by the United States in Kenya. Nevertheless, according to USAID officials, China's funding of infrastructure projects, through loans and grants, complements the U.S. government's focus on aid for poverty reduction. U.S. officials and other donors further observed that although China is invited to donor meetings, it does not actively coordinate its projects with other donors, preferring instead to work with host-country officials directly.

Host Governments Have Influenced U.S. and Chinese Engagement

Host-government requirements regarding foreign firms' use of local content—including employment of local workers—and expectations of foreign firms' exercising corporate social responsibility have influenced the United States' and China's respective engagement in the case-study countries.

□□ca□c□n□en□ Host-governments' local content requirements—which include employing local workers, partnering with domestic firms, and using local materials—have influenced U.S. and Chinese firms' engagement in these countries. For example, the Angolan government's requirement that foreign firms take local firms as partners has posed some challenges for U.S. firms, while the Ghanaian and Kenyan governments' strict requirements that foreign firms hire local workers have resulted in Chinese firms' hiring more local workers for construction projects in these countries.

- *Angola.* According to a 2012 report from State, for companies set up by national or foreign investors, the Angolan government limits the number of foreign employees to 30 percent of the workforce, effectively requiring that Angolans constitute 70 percent of the workforce.[111] In the petroleum sector, in addition to hiring local

---

[110]Comprehensive data on China's grants to Angola, Ghana, and Kenya are not available, in part because China does not publish country-specific aid data. The United States and other developed countries that are members of OECD are required to report aid data annually to OECD, which makes this information publicly available. China is not an OECD member and does not report such data.

[111]U.S. Department of State, *2012 Investment Climate Statement–Angola* (Washington D.C.: 2012).

workers or sourcing local products, oil service companies may meet Angola's local-content requirements by partnering with local Angolan firms.[112] According to U.S. officials, Angola's local-content requirements impede U.S. firms' ability to voluntarily choose their business partners. U.S. officials also noted that Angola's local-content requirements have raised concerns for some U.S. firms related to their responsibilities under the U.S. Foreign Corrupt Practices Act, which outlaws payments to foreign government officials to assist in securing or retaining business opportunities. According to U.S. officials, given the intertwining of Angolan private and government interests, complying with Angola's local content requirements could put U.S. companies in a position of having to partner with unknown, and potentially corrupt, entities. For instance, in one case a U.S. firm reported its partnership with an Angolan firm to U.S. officials after the U.S. firm became aware of links between the local firm and a senior Angolan government official, according to a U.S. official and information released by this firm. The Chinese government negotiated a lower local content requirement for Chinese firms implementing Chinese government–funded infrastructure projects, according to an Angolan NGO and reported statements by the former Chinese ambassador to Angola. According to these sources, the Chinese government's agreements with the Angolan government allow Chinese firms to use up to 70 percent foreign labor, and no less than 30 percent Angolan labor. However, these sources stated that Chinese firms generally were unable to meet the requirement to hire 30 percent of the workforce locally, in part because of a lack of skilled local workers in the years following Angola's civil war.

- *Ghana.* According to a 2012 report from State, Ghana's local content rules consist of a local-employment requirement for the retail sector. However, Ghana issues work permits for foreign workers in proportion to the size of the foreign firm's investment.[113] Moreover, according to U.S. officials, strong unions and greater public sensitivity to hiring practices limit the hiring of non-Ghanaian workers. Data from Ghana's

---

[112]The petroleum sector in Angola is subject to revised local content regulation, according to State. A 2008 decree by the Angolan government requires oil companies to first seek Angolan employees to fill any vacant position prior to seeking expatriate appointment, which must first be authorized by the Ministry of Petroleum.

[113]U.S. Department of State, *2012 Investment Climate Statement—Ghana* (Washington D.C.: 2012). This report also notes that Ghana requires foreign investors to have local partners in only a few sectors—fishing, insurance, and the extractive industries.

Ministry of Roads indicate that Ghanaian workers constitute the majority of workers hired by Chinese firms for construction projects.

- *Kenya.* Although the Kenyan government does not directly specify a minimum requirement for local employment, it encourages investments in sectors that create local employment, according to a 2012 report from State.[114] Additionally, the Kenyan government restricts the number of work permits for expatriate workers in foreign firms, according to officials from the Kenyan Private Investment Authority. As a result of these requirements, Kenya has restricted the number of Chinese workers, which has led to Chinese firms' hiring more local workers, according to U.S. and Kenyan government officials.

Corporate social responsibility. The Ghanaian and Angolan governments require firms in extractive industries, such as oil and other mining, to exercise corporate social responsibility by supporting philanthropic activities in the communities where they operate. For example, in the oil and diamond sectors, contracts with the Angolan government spell out the commitments companies must make to invest in infrastructure and social services to benefit local communities, such as building schools, equipping hospitals, or funding microcredit programs, according to State's investment climate report. Despite differences in U.S. and Chinese firms' roles in Angola's oil sector, where U.S. firms are mostly operators of oil blocks and Chinese firms are nonoperators, both contribute funds for community projects. Specifically, while U.S. and other oil companies in operator roles are held responsible for these activities, oil companies in nonoperator roles, such as Chinese firms in Angola, also contribute funds toward these philanthropic activities, according to a representative from a large western oil firm.

In addition to influencing U.S. and Chinese engagement, the governments of Ghana and Kenya have enhanced the transparency of Chinese government financing in their countries by publishing information

---

[114]U.S. Department of State, *2012 Investment Climate Statement—Kenya* (Washington D.C.: 2012).

about the scale, terms, and use of Chinese loans and grants.[115] Specifically, the Ghanaian government published the terms, such as the interest rate and fees, of its $3 billion loan agreement with China Development Bank and publishes annual budget reports that include information on the amount of Chinese government loans and grants for specific projects. Similarly, the Kenyan government annually publishes data on specific projects funded by the Chinese government.[116] In contrast, the Angolan government has published limited information on Chinese government loans. Specifically, the Angolan Ministry of Finance website lists projects as of 2008 that were funded through Chinese government credit lines issued in 2004 and 2007, but it has not published data on the terms of Chinese government credit lines and loans.

Concluding Observations

Assessing the implications of China's economic engagement in sub-Saharan Africa involves considerable challenges for U.S. policymakers. One such challenge is the limited availability of reliable information. While it is clear that China's economic engagement in the region has grown rapidly over the past decade, with China surpassing the United States as sub-Saharan Africa's leading trading partner, information on key aspects of that engagement is lacking. For example, unlike most global economic powers, China does not publish comprehensive data on its foreign assistance, or government-sponsored loans to the region. Our case-study analysis shows that additional information can, to some degree, be obtained by collecting available data on specific countries, but these data do not fully eliminate information gaps.

The information we obtained shows that, while both the United States and China are substantial oil importers from sub-Saharan Africa, their involvement across the region has differed in other respects. For example, the United States' emphasis on providing development assistance has been in contrast to China's active pursuit of increasing economic engagement through large-scale loans to governments for

---

[115]As a member of OECD's Development Assistance Committee, the U.S. government annually reports its data in disaggregated format for public reporting. Additionally, the OECD Arrangement on Export Credits requires participants such as U.S. Ex-Im to notify, consult with, and share information with other participants if U.S. Ex-Im offers loans on terms more generous than what the agreement specifies.

[116]The Kenyan government annually publishes reports on donor funding committed for the upcoming fiscal year. We were able to obtain these reports published from 2009 through 2011.

infrastructure projects, often involving the use of Chinese contractors. Available information from Angola, Ghana, and Kenya suggests that U.S. and Chinese firms generally operate in different and noncompeting sectors: U.S. firms are more concentrated in higher-technology areas, including petroleum exploration and production, and Chinese firms more concentrated in infrastructure. Increases in Chinese technological capacity could affect U.S. and Chinese commercial engagement in some sectors of sub-Saharan Africa in ways that are not easily known at this time.

Although not in direct response to China's engagement, the United States has recently elevated the importance of U.S. commercial engagement in its sub-Saharan Africa strategy, calling for increased trade and investment in the region. This reprioritization of U.S. goals reflects this region's prospects for economic growth as well as the perspective that advancing U.S. interests can benefit from a stronger integration of commercial goals with diplomatic engagement. Any increases in U.S. commercial engagement will take place in the context of policies that govern the ways in which the U.S. government can work to promote commercial interests, during a period of tight government budgets, and— as viewed by many U.S. firms—in the high-risk and high-cost business environments of many sub-Saharan African countries.

Agency and Third-Party Comments

We sent a draft of this report for review and comment to the Departments of Commerce, Defense, Energy, State, and the Treasury and to MCC, OPIC, USAID, U.S. Ex-Im, the U.S. Trade and Development Agency, and USTR. We received technical comments from Commerce, Energy, State, Treasury, OPIC, U.S. Ex-Im, and USTR, which we incorporated as appropriate. In addition, we sent relevant sections of the draft report to the World Bank, which also provided technical comments that we incorporated as appropriate.

We are sending copies of this report to the appropriate congressional committees; the Secretaries of Commerce, Defense, Energy, State, and the Treasury; the Chairman of U.S. Ex-Im; the Administrator of USAID; the United States Trade Representative; the Acting Director of the U.S. Trade and Development Agency; the Chief Executive Officers of OPIC and MCC; and other interested parties. The report also is available at no charge on the GAO website at http://www.gao.gov.

If you or your staff members have any questions about this report, please contact me at (202) 512-3149 or gootnickd@gao.gov. Contact points for our Offices of Public Affairs and Congressional Relations may be found on the last page of this report. GAO staff who made key contributions to this report are listed in appendix III.

David B. Gootnick,
Director, International Affairs and Trade

Appendix I: Objectives, Scope, and Methodology

Our objectives were to (1) examine U.S. and Chinese goals and policies for sub-Saharan Africa; (2) examine the United States' and China's trade, grants and loans, and investment activities for sub-Saharan Africa;[1] and (3) compare aspects of the United States' and China's engagement in selected case-study countries—Angola, Ghana, and Kenya.

To review U.S. and Chinese goals and policies with respect to sub-Saharan Africa, we reviewed U.S. government policies, plans, and legislation; publicly available Chinese government policies; and statements from U.S. government officials.

To examine the United States' and China's engagement with sub-Saharan Africa, including our case-study countries, we analyzed available data on U.S. and Chinese trade, grants and loans, and investments from 2001 through 2010 or 2011. To the extent that data were unavailable for this period, we used data for the most recent 3- to 5-year period available. To identify the best available data sources and any data limitations, we interviewed U.S. government officials and experts in Washington, D.C. We met with officials from the U.S. Agency for International Development (USAID); Departments of Commerce, Defense, Energy, State, and the Treasury; Export-Import Bank of the United States (U.S. Ex-Im); Millennium Challenge Corporation (MCC); Office of the U.S. Trade Representative (USTR); Overseas Private Investment Corporation (OPIC); and U.S. Trade and Development Agency. We also met with host-government officials, the World Bank, nongovernmental organizations (NGO), U.S. firms, business associations such as the Corporate Council on Africa and U.S.-Angola Chamber of Commerce, and experts from think tanks and academic institutions. We analyzed information on U.S. programs and funding from Commerce, MCC, OPIC, U.S. Ex-Im, and USAID. To describe China's engagement, we also assessed publicly available information from Chinese ministries, such as the Ministry of Commerce; the World Bank; the International Monetary Fund (IMF); the World Trade Organization; and scholarly literature. The information on foreign laws in this report is not a product of our original analysis but is derived from interviews and secondary sources.

To compare in greater depth aspects of the United States' and China's engagement in sub-Saharan Africa, we conducted case studies of

---

[1]We did not include security issues within the scope of this study.

Angola, Ghana, and Kenya. We selected these countries on the basis of an assessment of the levels, types, and intersection of the United States' and China's engagement in trade, grants and loans, and investment activity in each country; the three countries' geographic diversity; and input from U.S. government officials and relevant experts. These case studies are meant to be illustrative and are not generalizable.

- To obtain data on the United States' and China's trade in goods, we accessed the United Nations (UN) Commodity Trade database by means of the Department of Commerce's Trade Policy Information System. This database provides data for comparable categories of exports and imports of goods for the United States and China. For data on U.S. imports under the African Growth and Opportunity Act, we used Commerce's Trade Policy Information System. Although comparable data for trade in services were not systematically available for the United States and China, we cite relevant examples for services provided by U.S. and Chinese firms, using World Bank and MCC data on contracts for projects funded by these organizations in sub-Saharan Africa and using available data for U.S., Chinese, and other firms' bids for host-government contracts from Commerce's Advocacy Center. We also present our estimates of U.S. trade in services, based on tabulations from Commerce's Bureau of Economic Analysis (BEA) and other sources, including the Census Bureau. BEA's trade-in-services data for several categories of service—travel and passenger fares, transportation, education, and "other" private services—are based on data from various sources.[2] We used data on the number of Chinese laborers in Angola, from China's Ministry of Commerce and from a news report citing the former Chinese ambassador to Angola, as an indicator of China's service exports.

- To obtain data on the United States' grants and loans, we used data from USAID, U.S. Ex-Im, and OPIC. To obtain data on China's grants and aid, we used data from China's foreign aid policy and China scholar Deborah Brautigam. For country-specific data on China's grants and loans, we used data provided by U.S. government officials

---

[2]For example, to estimate travel and passenger fares, BEA uses data on passenger numbers collected by the Department of Homeland Security and tabulated by Commerce's International Trade Administration. To estimate numbers of students from sub-Saharan Africa countries who are studying in the United States and numbers of U.S. students studying in these countries, BEA uses data based an annual survey of accredited U.S. institutions conducted by the Institute for International Education.

and academic scholars and data published by host governments.

- For data on U.S. firms' investments, we used BEA data that we obtained directly from BEA. For Chinese firms' investments, we used data from China's Ministry of Commerce, China's National Bureau of Statistics, the information office of China's State Council, and Haver Analytics, as well as information on China's data from the IMF and academic experts. For U.S. and Chinese firms' investments in the oil sector in Angola and Ghana, we used data published by the governments of Angola and Ghana, with updates from the U.S. Department of Energy.

To ensure comparability, and given challenges in determining appropriate deflators for some data, we used nominal rather than inflation-adjusted values for U.S. and Chinese trade, grants and loans, and investments in sub-Saharan Africa. All of our information sources reported nominal data in U.S. dollars. All percentages noted in this document are rounded to the nearest number. We have noted data limitations as appropriate, such as limits in the availability of data on China's grants and loans and likely underreporting of its investment data. Overall, we determined that the data presented in this study are generally reliable for the purposes for which they are used. To assess the reliability of data, where possible, we cross-checked the data with other sources, conducted checks on the data for internal consistency, and consulted with U.S. officials and experts.

- We determined that trade-in-goods data for the United States and China were generally reliable for comparing trends over time as well as composition of trade. U.S. trade-in-services data represent broad estimates rather than precise values: values for certain services are extrapolated at the country level from broader data (e.g., travel service data are based on multiplying the number of travelers for a country with data on average expenditures for travelers and average passenger fees for the region), while values for other services (e.g., business, professional, and technical services) are calculated from a range of estimates based on survey data. In instances where the volume of trade for that service was presented as a range, we used the highest value to estimate the volume of trade for that service. China's trade-in-services data comprise data for Chinese imports and exports to the world, are not disaggregated by region or country, and cannot be compared with the U.S. data for sub-Saharan Africa and case-study countries. China's data also include data on the number of Chinese laborers in Africa and a few African countries, including Angola. The United States does not have comparable data on U.S. workers in Africa and in countries like Angola.

- In the absence of comparable U.S. and Chinese trade-in-services data, we analyzed data for contracts funded by the World Bank and MCC as well as data from Commerce's Advocacy Center on host-government contracts. Although these data represent a small share of services activity in the region, they provide insights into the degree of competition between U.S. and Chinese firms for the projects represented. We found that the data for contracts funded by the World Bank are generally reliable. We utilized data from MCC largely to provide information on the nature and extent of U.S. and Chinese firms' engagement in Ghana, and found the data to be generally reliable for that purpose. Commerce's Advocacy Center data were for a limited number of cases (47) where U.S. firms requested the agency's assistance in bidding for host-government contracts. Because these data included the nationality of other firms bidding on a host-government contract, we used this information to determine the extent to which Chinese firms or firms of other nationalities were competing with U.S. firms on these contracts. We did not use these data to determine the nationality of the winner for these contracts, because the data generally did not identify the nationality of the bidder.

- We determined that U.S. development assistance data are generally reliable for showing the trend and composition of aid to sub-Saharan African countries over time. We also determined that data from U.S. Ex-Im and OPIC are generally reliable to present trends and aggregate amounts by year, and we present these data with appropriate caveats. Since China does not publish aid data, we used the best available estimates of China's aid to Africa, produced by expert Deborah Brautigam. We did not independently verify Dr. Brautigam's data but obtained an understanding of the methodology she used to construct her estimates. We were unable to verify the reliability of data published by host-government ministries, but where possible, we asked for input from knowledgeable U.S. government officials. We have attributed to the appropriate sources information on Chinese government loans to the case-study countries and, to the extent possible, checked this information for consistency among the sources.

- To compare borrowers' costs for loans from the Chinese government with borrowers' costs for loans from other lenders, we analyzed data on loans provided by the Chinese government, the U.S. government, and the World Bank for similar sectors to the same countries for comparable periods. We obtained information on specific loans from U.S. officials, host-government officials and documents, the World

Bank, the Organization for Economic Cooperation and Development (OECD), an online source for the London Interbank Offered Rate (see www.fedprimerates.com), and an expert on China-Angola relations.[3] We collected publicly available information from the World Bank and verified loan terms with World Bank officials. To compare loans by U.S. and Chinese government agencies and the World Bank to the governments of Angola, Ghana, and Kenya, we collected and analyzed information on the terms of the loans (i.e., date of the loan agreement, face value of the loan, interest rate, repayment period, grace period, disbursement pattern, and fees). Chinese government loans included loans by the Export-Import Bank of China (China Ex-Im) and the China Development Bank supporting Chinese exports of goods and services. For these loans, we identified the borrowing country, the date of the loan agreement, the sector (primarily construction), and the face value, as benchmarks for collecting similar information for U.S. and World Bank loans. For U.S. government loans, we used information on U.S. Ex-Im loans that support U.S. exports of goods and services. Because U.S. Ex-Im did not provide loans for the construction sector to host governments during a similar period as the Chinese loans, we asked U.S. Ex-Im to provide hypothetical loan terms for loans that it might have offered for the construction sector on the same date and of the same magnitude as the Chinese government loans. We also collected information on the only two loans that U.S. Ex-Im provided to the government of one of our case-study countries, both of them to the government of Ghana, since 2001. For World Bank loans, when possible, we selected loans with publicly available information from the World Bank on loan terms and that were given for the construction sector during a similar period as the Chinese government loans. Because we could not find World Bank loans for the construction sector given in a similar period in Angola and Ghana, we used loans for the agriculture sector in Angola that included an infrastructure construction component and for the oil and gas sector in Ghana. To calculate the present value of the loan and repayment, we collected historical data on OECD's differentiated discount rate. Using this information, we calculated the loan's present value—that is the present value of future disbursements to the borrower, and we calculated the present value of future repayments to the lender for the life of the loan. We then used the ratio of the present

---

[3]See Lucy Corkin, "Angolan Political Elites' Management of Chinese Credit Lines," in Marcus Power and Ana C. Alves, eds., *China and Angola: A Marriage of Convenience?* (Capetown, South Africa: Pambazuka Press, 2012), 45-67.

value of repayment to the present value of the loan to calculate the loan's grant element—that is, the loan's concessionality.[4] Where necessary, we made assumptions to complete the calculations. For example, we assumed a disbursement period of 8 and a half years for China Ex-Im's November 2009 loan to Angola. We based this assumption on information from Angola's Ministry of Finance regarding a 2004 loan from China, which indicated that almost 50 percent of the loan had been disbursed as of 2008, about 4 and a quarter years after the loan agreement. Extrapolating this rate, we assumed that the loan would be fully disbursed 8 and a half years after the loan agreement. The IMF provides an online tool to calculate the grant element of the loan; however, we used a different methodology that allowed us to directly incorporate factors including the date of the loan, which affects the discount rate used to calculate the grant element. Using the IMF calculation tool could result in different calculations of the loans' grant elements.

- To identify patterns in, and to compare, U.S. and Chinese foreign direct investment, we report U.S. and Chinese data on foreign direct investments while noting their limitations. First, data on U.S. foreign direct investments in several countries were unavailable because of confidentiality concerns. Second, while both the United States' and China's foreign direct investment to sub-Saharan Africa may be underreported, experts have expressed particular concern regarding China's data. U.S. and Chinese firms set up subsidiaries in places such as Netherlands and the British Virgin Islands, which can be used to make investments in sub-Saharan Africa that are not captured by U.S. and Chinese data on foreign direct investment. Experts state that this could be a significant source of underreporting for China's data. In addition, U.S. and China's data may not include foreign direct investments from all firms. An IMF working paper expressed particular concern regarding foreign direct investments from China's small and medium-sized firms that are not captured in China's data.[5] For U.S. data, according to BEA, U.S. data on foreign direct investments are based on a benchmark survey conducted in 2009, BEA's most

---

[4]The higher the grant element, the more concessional the loan and the less the borrower has to repay relative to the amount borrowed. As a reference, donors who are OECD members define official development assistance to include loans for developmental purposes with a grant element of at least 25 percent.

[5]See Montfort Mlachila and Misa Takebe, "FDI from BRICs to LICs: Emerging Growth Driver?" *IMF Working Paper*, WP/11/178 (2011), 12.

comprehensive survey of U.S. foreign direct investment; this survey covers the value of all U.S. foreign direct investment and is the basis on which data for other years are compiled. Third, the flow data reported for China's foreign direct investment are inconsistent with changes in the stock data; according to the IMF working paper, these variations between flows and stock are difficult to explain.[6] U.S. foreign direct investment data do not show such levels of inconsistencies between the flow data and changes in the stock data. Fourth, China does not define foreign direct investment when reporting its data. However, the types of data included by China in its foreign direct investments (e.g., equity investment data, reinvested earnings data) appear similar to data reported for U.S. foreign direct investment, which the United States defines on the basis of OECD's definition of foreign direct investment.[7] Despite these limitations, various reports, including those published by international organizations such as the IMF, government agencies, academic experts, and other research institutions, use China's reported investment data to describe China's foreign direct investment activities in Africa. And despite U.S. foreign direct investment data being suppressed for some countries and some potential underreporting, we determined the U.S. foreign direct investment data to be reliable for reporting general patterns, when limitations are noted. Data on China's foreign direct investment by sector are reported by an official Chinese government source, and we have attributed these data as such. We have appropriately attributed data on U.S. and Chinese firms' investments in the oil sector in Angola and Ghana and have checked these data for consistency across sources to the extent available.

We conducted meetings in Washington, D.C., and fieldwork in Angola, Ghana, and Kenya, including meetings with officials from U.S. agencies; host-government ministries (e.g., those responsible for finance, foreign affairs, roads and urban development, energy, trade, and investment); U.S. businesses (representing sectors such as transportation, telecommunications, oil and gas, financial services, and agriculture); other donors; and nongovernmental organizations (e.g., think tanks, academic institutions, and advocacy organizations). We were unable to

---

[6]Mlachila and Takebe, "FDI from BRICs to LICs: Emerging Growth Driver?"

[7]According to the OECD, foreign direct investment is the ownership by a foreign person or business of 10 percent or more of the voting equity of a firm located in the host country.

meet with Chinese government officials, despite our requests in Africa and in Washington, D.C.

We conducted this performance audit from November 2011 to February 2013 in accordance with generally accepted government auditing standards. Those standards require that we plan and perform the audit to obtain sufficient, appropriate evidence to provide a reasonable basis for our findings and conclusions based on our audit objectives. We believe that the evidence obtained provides a reasonable basis for our findings and conclusions based on our audit objectives.

Appendix II: U.S. and Chinese Government Loans to Angola, Ghana, and Kenya

Our analysis of information on specific Chinese government loans to Angola, Kenya, and Ghana showed that these loans are generally less costly and more concessional than U.S. government loans to Angola, Kenya, and, to a lesser extent, Ghana. Our analysis also shows that these Chinese government loans are more costly than specific World Bank loans to Ghana and Kenya.[1]

To compare Chinese government loans with U.S. government and World Bank loans, we identified U.S. government and World Bank loans that were similar in agreement date, size, sector, and borrowing country. These factors affect a loan's interest rate, other associated fees, and duration. Because U.S. Ex-Im did not offer loans for the construction sector to the host government during a similar time period as the Chinese government loans, we obtained loan terms from U.S. Ex-Im for hypothetical loans for the construction sector on the same date and of the same magnitude as the Chinese government loans.[2] In instances where we could not obtain information about specific terms, we made assumptions based on the terms of comparable loans. We then compared Chinese government loans with those of the U.S. government and the World Bank based on the terms of the loans, such as their face value, interest rate, upfront fee, and repayment period, to calculate the loan's degree of concessionality or grant element, defined as the present value of future disbursements less the present value of future repayment (see table 3).[3] A positive difference between these two values indicates a grant element—a percentage of the loan that does not have to be repaid—and a negative difference indicates a negative grant element—a percentage of the loan that must be repaid in addition to the present value of the loan. The IMF provides an online tool to calculate the grant element of the loan; however, we used a different methodology that allowed us to

---

[1] The World Bank offers different types of loans to Angola compared to Ghana and Kenya.

[2] For the World Bank loans, we were unable to find loans of similar magnitude to the Chinese government loans. We were also unable to find loans that contained construction projects for Ghana with publicly available terms.

[3] In addition, we used information and assumptions regarding the disbursement period, disbursement pattern, grace period, the discount rate, commitment fees, repayment pattern, and agreement date to calculate the present value of the loan and of future repayment. For example, to discount future disbursement and repayment, we use the OECD's differentiated discount rate. This rate, recommended by the OECD to calculate the concessionality of loans for determining tied aid, is based on the official lending rates of OECD export credit agencies and a specified margin.

directly incorporate factors including the date of the loan, which affects the discount rate used to calculate the grant element. Using the IMF calculation tool could result in different calculations of the loans' grant elements than those shown in table 3.

Table 3: Comparison of Selected Chinese Government Loans with US Government and World Bank Loans to Angola, Ghana, and Kenya

Lender	Agreement Date	Face value (dollars in millions)	Interest rate (percent)	Up-front fee (percent)	Maturity (grace) period (years)	Present value of loan[a] (dollars in millions)	Present value of repayment[a] (dollars in millions)	Difference between present and repayment value (dollars in millions) (Grant element in percent)[b]
Angola								
China	November 2009	$6,000	3.22%	0.25%	28.5 (15)	$4,879	$4,064	$815 (17%)
China	November 2009	1,500	2.52	0.25	13 (8)	1,432	1,236	196 (14)
United States[c,d]	*November 2009*	*6,000*	*2.48*	*7.62*	*5.5 (5)*	*5,930*	*6,022*	*-91 (-2)*
World Bank[e]	November 2009	30	3.20[f]	None	34 (25)	24	21	3.2 (13)
Ghana								
China	December 2011	1,500	3.74	0.25	28.5 (15)	1,262	1,240	22 (2)
China	December 2011	1,500	3.64	0.25	21.5 (10)	1,262	1,244	18 (1)
United States[c]	*December 2011*	*1,500*	*2.45*	*10.15*	*15 (10)*	*1,356*	*1,360*	*-4 (-0.3)*
World Bank[e]	April 2011	38	0[f]	none	35 (25)	34	18	16 (48)
Kenya								
China	July 2011	45	2.00	0.25	35.5 (20)	38	27	10 (27)
United States[c]	*July 2011*	*45*	*3.51*	*17.37*	*15 (10)*	*41*	*46*	*-6 (-14)*
World Bank[e]	May 2011	300	0[f]	none	40 (30)	263	131	132 (50)

Source: GAO analysis of information obtained from U.S. officials, host governments, the World Bank, OECD, www.fedprimerates.com, and Lucy Corkin.

Notes: Italics indicate loans with a negative grant element—that is, loans whose present value of repayment exceeds its present value. While not listed in the table, each loan's commitment fee and disbursement period were used in the calculations of present values of the loan and repayment and of grant element. Face value and present values of the loan and repayment are reported in nominal values. London Interbank Offered Rates are drawn from www.fedprimerates.com. Lucy Corkin is an expert in China-Angola relations. See Lucy Corkin, "Angolan Political Elites' Management of Chinese Credit Lines," in Marcus Power and Ana C. Alves, eds., China and Angola: A Marriage of Convenience? (Capetown, South Africa: Pambazuka Press, 2012), 45-67.

[a]The present value of the loan reflects the present value of future disbursements of the loan. The loan is generally disbursed in increments over time.

[b]The grant element measures a loan's degree of concessionality.

[c]We assumed a hypothetical U.S. government loan, because the U.S. government had not made a loan to the host government for the construction sector during the same period as the Chinese government loan. The sector and the period when the loan is made affect the interest rate and other fees associated with that loan.

[d]U.S. Ex-Im did not make any long-term loans to the Angolan government during this period, according to U.S. Ex-Im officials. This hypothetical loan is a medium-term loan with shorter disbursement and repayment periods.

[e]For World Bank loans, we used the terms in the agreement (e.g., agreement date vs. effective date) for consistency with our calculations for U.S. and Chinese government loans. For the World Bank loan to Angola, according to World Bank officials, while the loan was initially negotiated at a 4.2 percent interest rate, the applicable interest rate was 3.2 percent when the agreement was signed.

[f]The World Bank charged a service fee of 0.75 percent in addition to the interest rate.

Our analysis indicates that the Chinese government loans to Angola, Ghana, and Kenya that we analyzed were generally more concessional than were hypothetical loans that U.S. Ex-Im might have offered. For example, two Chinese government loans to Angola in November 2009, for $6 billion and $1.5 billion, had estimated grant elements of 17 and 14 percent, respectively. In contrast, a loan that U.S. Ex-Im might have extended for the same time period would have had an estimated grant element of -2 percent, given U.S. Ex-Im terms that would apply to Angola. Because of higher upfront fees and a shorter repayment period, the repayment on the U.S. Ex-Im loan would have been higher than the repayment on the Chinese government loan.[4] By comparison, a World Bank loan to Angola in November 2009 had an estimated grant element of 13 percent, less concessional than the Chinese government loan but more concessional than the U.S. Ex-Im loan.[5] Two December 2011 Chinese government loans to Ghana and a July 2011 Chinese government loan to Kenya also had higher degrees of concessionality than hypothetical U.S. government loans to those countries. Table 4 shows the terms, present values of the loan and repayment, and grant

[4]Higher fees would not always result in a less concessional loan, if offset by other factors including lower interest rates.

[5]As a reference, according to the OECD, official development assistance includes loans for developmental purposes with a grant element of at least 25 percent. To determine whether a loan qualifies as official development assistance, a 10 percent discount rate is used to calculate the concessionality of the loan.

element for additional U.S. and Chinese government loans to Angola and Ghana.

Table 8: Additional U.S. and Chinese Government Loans to Angola and Ghana

Lender	Agreement Date	Face Value (Dollars in millions)	Interest rate (Percent)	Upfront fee (Percent)	Maturity (years) (Grace period in years)	Present Value of loan[b] (Dollars in millions)	Present value of repayment[b] (Dollars in millions)	Difference between present and repayment value (Dollars in millions) (Grant element in percent)[c]
Angola[a]								
China	March 2004	$2,000	2.61%	0.25%	25.5 (12)	$1,585	$1,149	$436 (27%)
China	*July 2007*	*500*	*6.61*	*0.25*	*13 (7)*	*485*	*492*	*-7 (-1)*
	September 2007	*2,000*	*6.74*	*0.25*	*28.5 (15)*	*1,529*	*1,583*	*-54 (-4)*
Ghana[d]								
United States[e]	October 2006	15	4.44	5.94	15 (15)	15	15	1 (4)
United States	*June 2008*	*358*	*4.45*	*20.26*	*16 (10)*	*300*	*331*	*-32 (-11)*

Source: GAO analysis of information obtained from U.S. officials, host governments, the World Bank, OECD, www.fedprimerates.com, and Lucy Corkin.

Notes: Italics indicate loans with a negative grant element—that is, loans whose present value of repayment exceeds their present value. While not listed in the table, each loan's commitment fee and disbursement period were used in the calculations of present loan value, present repayment value, and grant element. Face value, present loan value, and present repayment value are reported in nominal values. London Interbank Offered Rates are drawn from www.fedprimerates.com. Lucy Corkin is an expert in China-Angola relations. See Lucy Corkin, "Angolan Political Elites' Management of Chinese Credit Lines," in Marcus Power and Ana C. Alves, eds., China and Angola: A Marriage of Convenience? (Capetown, South Africa: Pambazuka Press, 2012), 45-67.

[a]U.S. Ex-Im did not make any loans to the Angolan government during this period, according to U.S. Ex-Im officials, and therefore U.S. Ex-Im did not provide terms for hypothetical loans that could be compared with Chinese government loans.

[b]The present value of the loan reflects the present value of future disbursements of the loan. The loan is generally disbursed in increments over time.

[c]The grant element measures a loan's degree of concessionality.

[d]These U.S. government loans to Ghanaian government represent the only two loans that U.S. Ex-Im has provided to a government of one of our case-study countries since 2001.

[e]According to U.S. Ex-Im, this loan was part of a tied-aid transaction in which U.S. Ex-Im provided a $7.8 million grant in addition to the loan shown. The terms shown represent only the loan component of this transaction. According to U.S. Ex-Im, this tied-aid transaction represented the only such transaction with a sub-Saharan African country since 2001.

Differences in each loan's interest rate; upfront fee; maturity, which includes the repayment, grace, and disbursement periods; and commitment fee drive the differences in the grant elements.

- *Interest rate.* For loans of similar time periods, the Chinese government loans charged higher interest rates than the U.S. government loans. Moreover, except in Angola, the World Bank charged much lower interest rates than both the U.S. government and the Chinese government. Higher interest rates increase repayments, decreasing the loan's grant element. Interest rates can vary depending on the borrowing country, sector, repayment period, and economic and political conditions, and other factors. For example, U.S. Ex-Im sets its interest rates on the basis of a minimum interest rate required by OECD that, in turn, is based on the U.S. Treasury bond rate, the loan repayment period, and the sector. According to U.S. Ex-Im officials, the Chinese government loans' interest rates reflect the risk of the borrower's defaulting on the loan and the cost of the funds, whereas the U.S. government loans' interest rates reflect only the cost of the funds.

- *Up-front fee.* U.S. Ex-Im loans follow the OECD rules for minimum exposure fees and carry substantially higher up-front fees than the Chinese government and the World Bank's loans.[6] Higher up-front fees increase repayments, decreasing the loan's grant element. According to U.S. Ex-Im officials, the up-front fee reflects the risk of the borrower's defaulting on the loan and is based on country risk, the terms of the loan, and the disbursement period. U.S. Ex-Im officials stated that, in contrast, the Chinese government loans' up-front fees do not include the risk of the borrower's defaulting on the loan and are similar to a transaction fee; instead, the loans' interest rates reflect the risk of the borrower's defaulting. According to U.S. Ex-Im officials, U.S. Ex-Im generally allows the borrower to pay the up-front fee as the loan is disbursed and generally provides a loan for the up-front fee that allows the borrower to repay the fee over a period of time.

- *Maturity.* A loan's maturity includes the repayment, grace, and disbursement periods. Only interest payments are made during the grace and disbursement periods, whereas both interest and principal repayments are made during the repayment period. The Chinese

---

[6]U.S. Ex-Im also calls the upfront fee the exposure fee.

government loans have longer repayment periods than the hypothetical U.S. government loans; the World Bank's loans have the longest repayment periods by far. Moreover, the Chinese government's and World Bank's loans offer grace periods, whereas the U.S. government loans do not. Longer repayment and grace periods allow for deeper discounting of future repayments, increasing the loan's grant element. Longer repayment and grace periods, which increase the loan's maturity, may also increase the discount rate used to calculate the present value of the loan and repayment, generally increasing the grant element. The disbursement period varies by loan, with longer disbursement periods decreasing both the loan and repayment value but generally increasing the grant element. Almost all of the loans in tables 3 and 4 are not disbursed fully at the onset of the loan but instead are disbursed over a period of time, sometimes over many years. U.S. government loans are disbursed as goods and services are delivered. Most of the Chinese government loans are used to fund infrastructure projects. According to experts, like U.S. government loans, the loans are disbursed as the Chinese firm implements the infrastructure project. In addition, the Chinese government loans are disbursed to the project's contractor, almost always a Chinese firm, keeping the loans' funds between the Chinese bank and the Chinese contractor.

- *Commitment fee.* The commitment fee for Chinese government loans is 1 percent, while the commitment fee for U.S. government and World Bank loans is .5 percent.[7] Commitment fees, which are charged on the amount of the loan that is not disbursed, increase the repayments, decreasing the loan's grant element. The impact of commitment fees grows with longer disbursement periods.

---

[7]World Bank officials review and approve the level of the commitment fee annually.

Appendix III: GAO Contact and Staff Acknowledgments

Contact	David Gootnick, (202) 512-3149 or gootnickd@gao.gov
Staff Acknowledgments	In addition to the contact named above, Celia Thomas (Assistant Director), Fang He, Farhanaz Kermalli, and Mona Sehgal made key contributions to this report. Gezahegne Bekele, Ming Chen, Lynn Cothern, David Dornisch, Mark Dowling, Philip Farah, Etana Finkler, Bruce Kutnick, Reid Lowe, Marc Molino, Mary Moutsos, and Jeremy Sebest provided technical assistance.

GAO's Mission	The Government Accountability Office, the audit, evaluation, and investigative arm of Congress, exists to support Congress in meeting its constitutional responsibilities and to help improve the performance and accountability of the federal government for the American people. GAO examines the use of public funds; evaluates federal programs and policies; and provides analyses, recommendations, and other assistance to help Congress make informed oversight, policy, and funding decisions. GAO's commitment to good government is reflected in its core values of accountability, integrity, and reliability.
Obtaining Copies of GAO Reports and Testimony	The fastest and easiest way to obtain copies of GAO documents at no cost is through GAO's website (http://www.gao.gov). Each weekday afternoon, GAO posts on its website newly released reports, testimony, and correspondence. To have GAO e-mail you a list of newly posted products, go to http://www.gao.gov and select "E-mail Updates."
Order by Phone	The price of each GAO publication reflects GAO's actual cost of production and distribution and depends on the number of pages in the publication and whether the publication is printed in color or black and white. Pricing and ordering information is posted on GAO's website, http://www.gao.gov/ordering.htm. Place orders by calling (202) 512-6000, toll free (866) 801-7077, or TDD (202) 512-2537. Orders may be paid for using American Express, Discover Card, MasterCard, Visa, check, or money order. Call for additional information.
Connect with GAO	Connect with GAO on Facebook, Flickr, Twitter, and YouTube. Subscribe to our RSS Feeds or E-mail Updates. Listen to our Podcasts. Visit GAO on the web at www.gao.gov.
To Report Fraud, Waste, and Abuse in Federal Programs	Contact: Website: http://www.gao.gov/fraudnet/fraudnet.htm E-mail: fraudnet@gao.gov Automated answering system: (800) 424-5454 or (202) 512-7470
Congressional Relations	Katherine Siggerud, Managing Director, siggerudk@gao.gov, (202) 512-4400, U.S. Government Accountability Office, 441 G Street NW, Room 7125, Washington, DC 20548
Public Affairs	Chuck Young, Managing Director, youngc1@gao.gov, (202) 512-4800 U.S. Government Accountability Office, 441 G Street NW, Room 7149 Washington, DC 20548

Please Print on Recycled Paper.

www.ingramcontent.com/pod-product-compliance
Lightning Source LLC
Chambersburg PA
CBHW080320290526
45790CB00005B/2113